the no-cry potty training solution

the no-cry potty training solution

Gentle Ways to Help Your Child
Say Good-Bye to Nappies

Elizabeth Pantley

Author of *The No-Cry Sleep Solution*

New York   Chicago   San Francisco   Lisbon   London   Madrid   Mexico City
Milan   New Delhi   San Juan   Seoul   Singapore   Sydney   Toronto

The No-Cry Potty Training Solution
Gentle ways to help your child say good-bye to nappies
Elizabeth Pantley

ISBN 10: 00 7 711551 1
ISBN 13: 978 007711551 7

Professional

Published by:
McGraw-Hill Publishing Company
Shoppenhangers Road, Maidenhead, Berkshire, England, SL6 2QL
Telephone: 44 (0) 1628 502500
Fax: 44 (0) 1628 770224
Website: www.mcgraw-hill.co.uk

British Library Cataloguing in Publication Data
A catalogue record of this book is available from the British Library.

McGraw-Hill books are available at special quantity discounts. Please contact the corporate sales executive.

This book is designed to provide parents and caregivers with a variety of ideas and suggestions. It is sold with the understanding that the publisher and the author are not rendering psychological, medical or professional services. It is also sold with the understanding that the author is not a doctor or psychologist and that the information in this book is the author's opinion, unless otherwise stated. Questions and comments attributed to parents represent a compilation and adaptation of many reader letters, unless indicated otherwise. This material is presented without any warranty or guarantee of any kind, express or implied, including but not limited to the implied warranties of merchantability or fitness for a particular purpose. It is not possible to cover every eventuality in any answer, and the reader should always consult a professional for individual needs. Readers should bring their child to a doctor or medical care provider for regular checkups and bring any questions they have to a medical professional. In regards to every topic included herein, this book is not a substitute for competent professional health care or professional counselling.

Printed and bound in Great Britain by Bell & Bain Ltd., Glasgow

Mixed Sources
Product group from well-managed forests and other controlled sources
www.fsc.org Cert no. TT-COC-002769
© 1996 Forest Stewardship Council

The *McGraw·Hill* Companies

This book is dedicated to the Test Mummies and Test Daddies who have worked with me on my No-Cry books: Sleep, Potty, and Discipline. Each and every one of you holds a very special place in my heart. It is a joy to know that while you come from all different types of families, and from all corners of the world, we share the same goals, the same ideals and the same heart.

I enjoy our many exchanges and I learn so much from you and your children. I sincerely appreciate your willingness to share and your enthusiastic commitment to help other parents through the challenging and rewarding parenting journey. And I cherish every photo you send of your little darlings.

Thank you for everything.

I'm sending warm hugs to you and to your children.

Contents

Acknowledgements

With warm and heartfelt appreciation to:

- Judith McCarthy and everyone at McGraw-Hill, absolutely the best publisher ever
- Meredith Bernstein, agent extraordinaire
- Patti Hughes, incredible, enthusiastic assistant
- My family, my joy: Robert, Mum, Angela, Vanessa, David, Coleton, Michelle, Loren, Sarah, Nicholas, Renée, Tom, Matthew, Devin, Tyler, Amber and Mike

And to my wonderful group of Test Mummies and Test Daddies: Jen, Jodie, Mel, Shelia, Amy, Tina, Angela, Sarah, Patti, Genevieve, Janie, Sharon, Rina, Lucie, Tracy, Rhonda, Kathi, Bridget, Molly, Ezia, Michelle, Matthew, Lorraine, Romi, Tonia, Kirsten, Leanne, Sheri, Kara, Diana, Liz, Kieron, Sean, Jocelyn, Bethany, Julie, Bonnie, Toni, Jennifer, Greg, Stephanie, Gabriela, Marianne, Shaila, Shelley, Linda, Olga, Rachael, Kim, Jane, Jolene, Asphyxia, Deborah, Kari, Brianna, Tiane, Gary, Xenia, Rebecca, Christy, Frances, Avital, Ann, Angelique, Annette, Renee, Beckie, Sheila, Carole, Karen, Annik, Deanna, Linda, Mari, Pamela, Catherine, Monica, Isadora, Yolanda, Louise, Michael, Margaret, Lorna, Loddie, Ashlea, Ryan, David, Liat, Kristi, Leigh, Lisa, Nikki, Wendy, Keelin, Tracy, Janice, Tara, Deandra, Luke, Krista, Josef, Mark, Juliana, Sarah, Jesse, Suzanne, Kristi, Christine, Karen,

Faith, Marisa, Diana, Janice, Theresa, Wanda, Kia, Brian, Janell, Christina, Doreen, Jaimie, John, Ole, Sherry, Joanne, Sara, Amy, Marie, Jacquelyn, Barbara, Mara, Nicole, Ric, Rivka, Yenny, Graeme, Alan, Brandy, Amy, Marcie, Anne-Marie, Kendra, Andreia, Kendra 2, Donna, Juliane, Sherisse, Andrew, Noreen, Reneé, Josh, Adam, Stacey, Julietta, Louise, Reagan, Felicia, Jessica, Jim, Marianna, Phylicia, Debbie, Tiffany, Maribel, Bruce, Daniel, Amy, Melissa, Monica, Sekou, Rachelle, Sonja, Lindsay, Cristina, Bobbie, Christy, Nicole, Oliver, Becky, Ann, Catherine, Osama, Barb, Kim, Natasha, Catherine, Jennifer, Amy, Bobbie, Keara, Elana, Sakina, Gale, Michelle, Graciela, Ken, Britt, Bill, Eleese, Maisha, Karen, Sarah, Laura, Amanda, Mike, Marlo, Judy, Christy, Erin, Joe, Meleila, Cindy, Liz, Betsy, Karolyn, Myles, Kimberly, Jacqueline, Adam, Natalia, Esther, Jessie, Michel, Sharalyn, Karen, Dale, Margaret, Melvin, Mary, Lynee, Heidi

Introduction

Potty training your child shouldn't require an instruction manual the size of a telephone book, nor should it require a visit to your doctor. It certainly shouldn't involve a paediatrician's assistance! Yet you may be like many other parents who get the idea that this is a complicated, difficult undertaking and can't possibly be done with ease. I have good news. As a parent educator and four-time veteran of the toilet training process, I know that potty training *can* be simple, pleasant and, yes, even fun. I've written this guide so that you can sail through the potty training process easily and joyfully with your child.

The No-Cry Potty Training Quick Guide

The first thing you'll find in this book is a six-part Quick Guide to potty training. This is a summary of the high points in this book. It offers everything you need to know to get your child from nappies to underpants. It's simple because potty training should be simple. I'd like to help you eliminate any tense emotions, competitiveness, and analysis before we even get started, as these unnecessarily complicate the process. If you'll follow a few straightforward steps, your child can pleasantly achieve the move out of nappies without stress or tears.

Relax: It's Simply Natural

You've been going to the toilet for a long, long time, and it's something you do without much thought. Your child has been using a nappy for a long time, and it's something he or she does without much thought. For the first time, your child will learn to listen to his or her body signals and think about getting to the toilet on time. This will be a big change in your child's everyday life, and it's a step towards independence that young children embrace. It's something that every child adjusts to in time, and it's a process that most children enjoy learning.

When you approach toilet training with knowledge, respect, patience and a plan, it can be as normal and uncomplicated as teaching your child how to walk, talk or use a spoon. This can be a wonderful learning experience for both of you.

So here we go. Have fun with potty training!

The No-Cry Potty Training Solution Quick Guide

The following Quick Guide will provide you with an overview of the toilet training process. It can serve as an introduction to or a review of the potty training plan, or as a reminder once you've set up your child's toilet training plan. The Quick Guide highlights the information contained in the rest of this book, so when you need more details you can easily refer to the corresponding expanded chapter.

Quick Guide 1:
Facts About Potty Training

Potty training can be natural, easy and peaceful. The first step is to know the facts.

- The perfect age to begin potty training is different for every child. Your child's best starting age could be anywhere from eighteen to thirty-two months. Pre-potty training preparation can begin when a child is as young as ten months.
- You can begin training at any age, but your child's biology, skills and readiness will determine when he can take over his own toileting.

Jordan, two years old

- No matter the age that toilet training *begins*, most children become physically capable of independent toileting between ages two and a half and four.
- It takes three to twelve months from the start of training to daytime toilet independence. The more readiness skills that a child possesses, the quicker the process will be.
- The age that a child masters toileting has absolutely no correlation to future abilities or intelligence.
- Night-time dryness is achieved only when a child's physiology supports this—you can't rush it.
- A parent's readiness to train is just as important as a child's readiness to learn.
- Most toddlers urinate four to eight times each day, usually about every two hours or so.
- Most toddlers have one or two bowel movements each day, some have three, and others skip a day or two in between movements. In general, each child has a regular pattern.

- More than 80 per cent of children experience set-backs in toilet training.
- Ninety-eight per cent of children are completely daytime independent by age four.

For more information, read Chapter 1.

Quick Guide 2:
Readiness Quiz

Potty training is easier and happens faster if your child is ready. Take this quiz to find out where your child is on the readiness spectrum. (An expanded quiz appears in Chapter 2.)

1. I can tell by watching that my child is wetting or filling his nappy:
   a. Never.
   b. Sometimes.
   c. Usually.
2. My toddler's nappy needs to be changed:
   a. Frequently, every hour or two.
   b. It varies.
   c. Every two to three hours—sometimes less frequently.
3. My child understands the meaning of *wet, dry, clean, wash, sit* and *go*:
   a. No.
   b. Some of them.
   c. Yes.
4. When my child communicates her needs, she:
   a. Says or signs a few basic words and I guess the rest.

      b. Gets her essential points across to me.
      c. Has a good vocabulary and talks to me in sentences.

5. If I give my child a simple direction, such as, "put this in the toy box," she:
      a. Doesn't understand or doesn't follow directions.
      b. Will do it if I coach or help her.
      c. Understands me and does it.

6. My child can take his trousers off and put them on:
      a. No.
      b. With help he can.
      c. Yes.

7. I think that it's the right time to begin potty training my child:
      a. No.
      b. I'm undecided.
      c. Yes.

Total the number of responses for each letter:

    a. _____
    b. _____
    c. _____

Most answers are *a*: *Wait*.
Your little one doesn't seem to be ready just yet. Test again in a month or two.

Most answers are *b*: *Time for pre-potty training—get ready!*
Your child is not quite ready for active training, but you can take steps to prepare your toddler for the future. Gradual introduction of terms and ideas will make potty training easier.

Most answers are c: *Your toddler is ready to use the potty!*
It's time to start your potty training adventure.

Between two scores
Just like any parenting situation, there are choices to make. If your child is hovering between two categories, your intuition and knowledge of your own child can direct you towards the right plan of action.

For more information and the expanded quiz, read Chapter 2.

Quick Guide 3:
Pre-Potty Training

If your child is near or past his first birthday, you can begin incorporating these ideas into his life. They are simple things that will lay the groundwork for potty training and will make the process much easier when you're ready to begin.

- During nappy changes, narrate the process to teach your toddler the words and meanings for toilet-related functions, such as *wee* and *poo*. Include descriptive words that you'll use during the process, such as *wet*, *dry*, *wipe* and *wash*.
- If you're comfortable with it, bring your child with you when you use the toilet. Explain what you're doing. Tell him that when he gets bigger, he'll put his wee and poo in the toilet instead of in his nappy. Let him flush the toilet if he wants to.

- Help your toddler identify what's happening when she wets or fills her nappy. Tell her, "You're going poo in your nappy." Have her watch you dump and flush.
- Start giving your child simple directions and help him to follow them. For example, ask him to get a toy from another room or to put the spoon in the dishwasher.
- Encourage your child to do things on her own: put on her socks, pull up her trousers, carry a cup to the sink, or fetch a book.
- Have a daily sit-and-read time together.
- Take the quiz again in a month or two to see if you're ready to move on to active potty learning.

For more information, read Chapter 3.

Quick Guide 4: It's Potty Time!

Get Ready
- Buy a potty, a dozen pairs of training pants, four or more elastic-waist trousers or shorts, and a supply of pull-ups or disposables with a feel-the-wetness sensation liner.

Get Set
- Put the potty in the bathroom, and tell your child what it's for.
- Read books about going on the potty to your child.
- Let your child practise just sitting on the potty without expecting a deposit.

Go

- Begin dressing your child in training pants or pull-ups.
- Create a potty routine—have your child sit on the potty when she first wakes up, after meals, before getting in the car, and before bed.
- If your child looks like she needs to go—tell, don't ask! Say, "Let's go to the potty."
- Boys and girls both can learn sitting down. Teach your son to hold his penis down. He can learn to stand when he's tall enough to reach.
- Your child must relax to go: read a book, tell a story, sing or talk about the day.
- Make hand washing a fun part of the routine. Keep a step stool by the sink, and have colourful, child-friendly soap available.
- Praise her when she goes!
- Expect accidents, and clean them up calmly.
- Matter-of-factly use nappies or pull-ups for naps and bedtime.
- Either cover the car seat or use pull-ups or nappies for car trips.
- Visit new bathrooms frequently when away from home.
- Be patient! It will take three to twelve months for your child to be an independent toileter.

Stop

- If your child has temper tantrums or sheds tears over potty training, or if you find yourself getting angry, then stop training. Read this book, particularly Chapters 7 and 8, and try again in a month or two.

For more information, read Chapters 4 and 5.

Quick Guide 5:
Bed-Wetting

- Young children wet the bed for biological reasons: his kidneys aren't sending a signal to his brain while asleep, his bladder hasn't grown large enough to hold a full night's supply of urine, or he sleeps so deeply he doesn't wake up to go to the toilet.
- You can't teach a child to be dry at night until his physiology allows this—it is not under his control.
- Never wake your child to take him to the toilet. You'll just disturb his sleep.
- It's normal. Half of all three-year-olds and 40 per cent of four-year-olds wet the bed several times a week. Also, 20 to 25 per cent of five-year-old children and 10 to 15 per cent of six-year-olds don't stay dry every night.
- Bed-wetting is hereditary, so if one or both parents were bed wetters, a child has a much greater chance of being one.
- For a bed-wetting toddler or preschooler, the solution is simple: have your child use the potty before bed, and then have him sleep in a nappy, padded training pants, or disposable absorbent pull-ups. When he has a week of dry mornings, it's time to change to underpants and use a mattress cover until he consistently stays dry all night.
- You only need to talk to a doctor about bed-wetting if your child is seven years of age or older or if there are other symptoms of a sleep disorder, such as loud, frequent snoring, or symptoms of an infection, such as painful elimination.

For more information, read Chapter 6.

Quick Guide 6:
Solving Common Toilet Training Problems

Problem	Reasons Why It Happens	Solutions
Your child shows readiness but won't try.	• She doesn't understand. • The process is not interesting enough. • She is going through a negative phase.	• Re-evaluate your approach, and try something new. • Have a few step-by-step lessons and make it fun. • Put up a sticker poster or put a bowl of small prizes in the bathroom and award one for each use.
Your child has lots of accidents.	• He is distracted. • He is not noticing his body's warning signs.	• Set a timer to ring every two hours. Take him to the potty when it rings. • Help him identify his need to go. ("You're wiggling; let's go on the potty.")
Your child is constipated.	• There are problems with her diet. • She does not have the patience to sit on the potty. • She is feeling pressure about training. • She is holding it too long.	• Increase fruit, vegetables, whole grains and water. Avoid refined sugar, sweets, fizzy drinks, cheese, rice and junk food. • Relax the potty training a bit. • Teach her to go as soon as she needs to go.
Your child won't poo on the potty.	• It feels wrong to him to use the toilet after going in a nappy for so long. • He is fearful about the process. • He's not yet able to read his body's warning signals.	• Reassure him that he's learning and soon he'll have his BMs in the potty. • Have him poo in the toilet, even if it's in his nappy. • Clean him in the bathroom, wipe him on the potty, and have him flush.

(continued)

Problem	Reasons Why It Happens	Solutions
Your child won't poo on the potty. (cont.)	• He had a bad experience, such as constipation or a fall off the toilet.	• Get a soft, padded toilet seat. • Don't personalize his stool by talking to it. • Line the potty bowl with a nappy or cut the crotch out of a nappy and have him sit and try to go. • Read, sing or tell stories when he is on the potty. Play soft music to help him relax.
Your child won't use the potty at nursery.	• She relies on parent prompts at home. • Different routines are confusing to her. • She is not comfortable with the bathroom. • She gets too busy playing.	• Practise each morning when you drop her off at nursery. • Have routine potty times. • Set a plan with your day care provider. • Ask your child what will help.
Your child uses the potty at nursery or the childminder's but not at home.	• The nursery schedule or method creates success. • Peer pressure motivates him to go.	• Ask the nursery staff for tips. • Use the nursery schedule at home. • Duplicate the childminder's method at home. • Create a sticker chart for your child to use.
Your child won't go when away from home.	• She has stage fright. • She doesn't understand that she's supposed to. • She can't relax when away from home. • She is embarrassed. • She's not used to a big toilet.	• Bring along a book to read. • Visit the potty everywhere you go. • Teach her a private signal or word to tell you when she has to go. • Tell her that everyone uses toilets everywhere you go.

(continued)

Problem	Reasons Why It Happens	Solutions
Your child won't go when away from home. *(cont.)*	• She doesn't understand why you cover or clean the seat, or she is scared of the germs.	• Bring a portable folding toilet seat cover. • Don't dwell on germs. Tell her that you cover or clean the seat because it's not your own toilet.
Your child was trained but has regressed.	• A life change is causing stress. • He has lost interest. • You stopped reminding him. • He has a medical problem.	• Give extra love and praise. • Take him to the potty at routine times. • Introduce a sticker chart or potty prizes. • Talk to your doctor.
You are getting impatient and angry.	• Things are not progressing according to plan. • You have unreasonable expectations.	• Read books and articles about potty training. • Talk to other, experienced parents. • Talk to your doctor. • Stop training for a month or so and regroup.

It isn't always easy to determine the reason for a problem, and solutions are not always simple. For more information, read Chapters 7 and 8.

1

Potty Training: What's It All About?

At the start of the grand adventure that is teaching a child to use the toilet, many parents wonder how they'll ever accomplish such a complex feat. They watch their toddler with his brand-new potty on his head and doubt the sanity that convinced them to purchase it in the first place. The good news is that the vast majority of children are able to master daytime toileting by the age of three and a half or so, and for most families it's a pleasant, even fun experience.

Take a moment to think about how you teach your child other new life skills. How do you teach your child to recite the alphabet, draw a picture, tie his shoes, dress himself, or put together a puzzle? Do you spend one full day on intense lessons and then expect your child to pass a test at the end of the day? Would you insist that he show mastery every day thereafter without ever making any mistakes? I doubt it! If you did approach lessons in this way, you'd likely end up frustrated and your child would be in tears.

The actual way that we teach children new skills is by doing it gradually, over a period of months, celebrating every little victory along the way. This doesn't apply just to toddlers—it's a pattern you'll follow for many years to come with your child, from the first new bicycle, to the brand-new driver's licence, and about a million other new things in between.

Think about *your part* in your child's learning processes. How do you act when teaching your child something new? Are you intense and emotional? Do you insist that he sit still and pay attention? Do you put a crayon in his hand and demand that he work, while you sit and worry that he'll never learn to draw a proper picture or print a capital A? Do you think you'll be sitting next to him, taking notes, when he goes to school? Do you fret that he'll be wearing Velcro shoes to senior school or you'll have to button his jacket for him on his wedding day? Of course not! You know that your child will master these skills—and many, many more—during his lifetime and that teaching him is one of your roles as a parent.

Consider your *expectations* when teaching your child something new. When teaching him to draw a picture, what do you expect will be the first thing he'll put down on paper? A family portrait? No, it's a scribble! And you'll delight in his effort and post his artwork on the refrigerator door. Over time, and with practice, that scribble will take shape until eventually your child will draw circles and squares and soon houses, people and animals.

Now think about this next new event in your child's life: toilet training. You can, and should, approach toilet training the same way that you do any other new skill—step-by-step, over time, with joy, kindness and patience.

Keep Things in Perspective

Not only is there no need to rush the process, but rushing things can lead to disaster. It puts tremendous stress on both you and your child. It makes the whole process a miserable experience instead of the ordinary learning process that it should be. Even more, when stress and pressure enter the picture, it can create resistance, tantrums, constipation, excessive accidents and setbacks.

Your child will learn to use the toilet. She'll learn best in her own way and on her own time schedule. There is no prize for the most quickly trained child. And research proves over and over that early or late toileting mastery has nothing whatsoever to do with how smart or capable a child is. So relax and enjoy the process.

When to Start

You can *begin* toilet training a child at any age: you can even sit a newborn baby on the potty. However, the more important question is when will training be finished? A child will *complete* toilet training when his biology, skills and development have matured to a point that he is capable and willing to take over complete control of his toileting. Only then can he recognize the need to go, stop his play, go to the toilet, handle the entire process, and return to his play.

The amount of time it takes for your child to master toilet training is closely related to the span between the

Elliot-Rose, ten months old

age when you start training and the age that he is physically and emotionally able to take responsibility. A number of studies show that no matter the age that toilet training *begins*, the majority of children are only physically capable of independent toileting after age two, and mastery usually happens between ages two and a half and four.

What About Starting Early—Before Readiness?

A child can be put on the toilet even as an infant, and in some cultures this is routinely done. A small percentage of parents have adopted this practice, called elimination communication (EC). Before you sign up thinking your life just got a whole lot easier, you need to know that EC is *not* potty training. It is a long-lasting, gentle, gradual system that is used instead of nappies to manage a child's waste. It replaces hourly nappy changes with hourly visits to the potty.

With this method, parents read their baby's body language and sound cues and put her on a potty when they think it is time for her to eliminate. The parent manages the child's elimination process until the child is physically capable of total independent toileting— which usually happens at that magical age span we talked of earlier: from two and a half to four.

If the idea of replacing nappies with a programme of watching your child's signals and placing her on a potty to eliminate appeals to you, then look up one of the many books on the topic of elimination communication, also called infant potty training. In *The No-Cry Potty Training Solution*, we'll approach toilet training from the more common toddler-readiness approach.

Can You Do It in a Day?

For the majority of families who consider toilet training a toddler event, some will look for a fast-fix solution. However, even those appealing books or programmes that promise one-day results have a major stipulation: they recommend using the ideas *only* when a child shows all the signs of readiness *and* is at a starting age of about two years. They also warn that accidents may occur for months afterwards and the parent must be diligent to continue taking the child to the toilet on a frequent basis.

Father-Speak

"We tried the 'get a doll that wets and potty train in a day' routine. Unfortunately, Hadley was more interested in eating the chips, drinking the juice, and playing with the doll than learning anything at all about potty training. The ritualistic sits on the potty quickly became full-blown tantrums, after which she'd wee on the floor. Now she hates her potty, and we're going to buy a new one and try a more gradual process."

—**Mark, father of twenty-eight-month-old Hadley**

Also, most children don't respond to one-day training with total success at day's end. Instead, it acts as a catalyst for the months of training that follow.

Can This Be a Child-Led Decision?

When deciding when to start potty training, you will certainly want to consider your child's readiness and interest. However, if you wait until that magic day when your child approaches you with a formal request to begin toilet training, you may be waiting a long, long, *long* time. A child simply doesn't understand the value of moving out of nappies to toilet independence. A child doesn't have the experience, knowledge, references or wisdom to make this kind of decision on his own.

Think about it. Do you let your child decide his own bedtime? Do you let him take the lead on when he'll dress himself (be prepared to be his valet until he reaches primary school!). Will you allow him to decide when he's ready to begin nursery?

Your child counts on you to make many decisions for him. Even though he'd like to go to bed at 10 P.M., you decide that when he's tired and yawning at 7 P.M. that's a much better choice. And while he may want to go to school with his older brother, you know that he's nowhere near ready.

One of your important roles as a parent is to make decisions for your child until she is ready to make them on her own. When it comes to toilet training, she needs you to watch her for readiness cues and then for you to introduce this novel concept to her when you feel she's ready to embrace it. And you are very qualified to make this decision, because you probably know your child better than she knows herself.

Potty Training Is Really Potty Learning

The terms *potty training* and *toilet training* have been around forever and are the terms that most people use to describe the process. However, it's not really about training at all—it is about teaching and learning. So a more accurate label for the process would be *potty learning* or *toilet teaching*. With this in mind, I polled more than three hundred parents about their choice of terms. While all of them agreed it is really about *learning*, 94 per cent felt much more comfortable with the traditional names and said that if they were looking for a book on the topic, they would search the common phrases. So throughout this book, I'll stick with the time-honoured terms *potty training* and *toilet training*—but as you and I both know, it's a teaching/learning process.

How Long Will It Take a Toddler to Learn?

When toilet training begins at about age two, it can take anywhere from three to twelve months from the start of potty training to daytime toilet independence. As a rule, the younger the child is and the fewer readiness skills she possesses, the more a parent must be involved and the longer the training process will take.

No matter what your approach to potty training, 98 per cent of children are completely daytime independent by age four. (Night-time dryness is a separate issue, based on physiology, and can take much longer.)

It's Not All or Nothing, You Know!

Toilet training isn't necessarily an all-or-nothing decision. Many parents begin the process early with their child because they would rather assist, remind and clean up a few accidents than continue to change nappies. Some decide to start slowly and watch their child's signs to progress to each new level. Others focus intently on training with hopes they can move things along quickly.

Any path you choose for your little one can work, as long as you are positive and patient. No matter your plan, it does take time to go from nappies to total independence. For many parents, halfway in between isn't a bad place to be, even if they spend six months at that midpoint.

Parenting is filled with choices, and the final decisions are very different for every family. There isn't just one right way to potty train a child—the variations, approaches and methods are many. The right approach for you is the one that feels right to you and works for you and your child. Ultimately, you'll need to evaluate what your family goals are and then set a plan that works best for you.

How Much Will Potty Training Cost?

There is an enormous market for potty training paraphernalia, such as expensive dolls that drink and wet, specially made potties, tot-sized urinals, fancy charts, posters, prizes and awards. While all of these can certainly make for a fun experience, it's not at all necessary to purchase an array of products for such a simple, natural process.

A potty, a dozen pairs of training pants, and a relaxed and pleasant attitude are all that's really needed to teach your child how to use the toilet. Anything extra is truly optional.

Helpful Facts to Know

You probably don't think much about your own elimination process, and it's probably been a while since the colour and consistency of your child's nappy deposits

Halene, fifteen months old

have been part of your daily conversation. (Remember those days?) There are some facts that are helpful to know as you embark on the toilet training journey.

- Toilet training has nothing to do with night-time dryness. Night-time dryness is achieved only when a child's physiology supports this. A child wets during sleep because of a number of reasons: his kidneys aren't sending a signal to his brain when he's asleep to alert him he has to go, his bladder hasn't yet grown large enough to contain a full night's supply of urine, his bladder overproduces urine during the night, or he sleeps so deeply he doesn't wake up to go to the toilet. As children grow, all of these conditions are self-correcting. This usually occurs between the ages of three and six. This isn't something you can teach, and you can't rush it. (See Chapter 6, on bed-wetting.)

• A parent's readiness to train is just as important as a child's readiness to learn. A child can't learn how to use the toilet unless someone teaches her. And the teacher's approach and attitude can have a direct effect on how long the process takes and how pleasant the journey is. A parent who is stressed about the process or who is too busy to dedicate the time necessary for teaching can slow the process or even bring it to a screeching halt. Conversely, a knowledgeable, patient parent with a pleasant approach can make the process enjoyable and bring much better, quicker results.

• Most toddlers urinate four to eight times each day, usually about every two hours or so. A child's bladder can hold about 30 to 40 ml of urine for each year of age. (A two-year-old's bladder can hold about 50 to 90 ml; a three-year-old's, about 90 to 130 ml; and a four-year-old's, about 120 to 180 ml—less than a cup.)

• Most toddlers have one or two bowel movements each day, some have three, and others skip a day or two in between movements. In general, each child has a regular pattern.

• A child's diet will affect the amount and frequency of urination and bowel movements. Adequate daily liquids, including water, plus a healthy diet containing foods with plenty of fibre (fruit, vegetables and whole grains) will make elimination easier—which in turn makes potty training easier.

• Ample daily exercise ensures that your child's stool is moved through her system properly. Lack of movement can contribute to constipation.

• A child's pelvic and sphincter muscles need to relax in order to release wee or poo. Stress, pressure or anxiety is a surefire way to stop the process. (That's why some children go in their nappy immediately after they are taken off the toilet.)

• Polls have shown that more than 80 per cent of parents say that their children experience setbacks in toilet training. This high number indicates that what we often label as "setbacks" is really just the usual path to mastery of toileting. Just like any new thing that children learn, it's not always a direct arrow from start to finish. It's often more like a squiggly line, with bursts of success as well as snags and pauses along the way to the final result.

• No matter what approach is used for toilet training, 98 per cent of children are completely daytime independent by age four.

2

The Readiness Quiz: Is It Time for Potty Training?

When you and your child are both truly ready for potty training, it can be an easy and pleasant experience. But the big question is, how do you know when you're ready? If you have never travelled this road before, you likely don't even know what signs to look for.

The Readiness Factor

There are three areas of readiness skills: physical, cognitive and social. A child who has always eliminated into a nappy without giving it much thought has many new things to learn. In addition, there are many motor skills involved in the actual process. And even more, a young child doesn't truly understand the benefits of moving out of nappies, because she's never lived that way.

The Parent's Role

When a child is ready to learn how to use the potty, it's important that the parent be ready and willing to embark on the training process and that the timing is

What It Takes to Master Toilet Training

For a child to be independent in the potty department, she must be able to do the following:

- Identify the body signals that indicate a full bladder or bowel.
- Remember that her lifetime routine has changed and that she should not go in her nappy.
- Understand that she must stop her current activity and use the toilet when she feels the urge to go.
- Control the holding of urine and stool until the time and place are right.
- Communicate the need to use the toilet.
- Walk to the potty, pull down her trousers, and sit on the toilet.
- Control the releasing of urine and stool into the toilet.
- Have enough patience to wait for elimination to occur.
- Wipe with the right amount of toilet paper, get off the toilet, flush, and pull up her trousers.
- Get up to the sink and wash and dry her hands.
- *Remember* the steps to using the toilet: the when, where and how.
- Have enough interest, motivation and patience to follow all of these steps five to eight times a day, every day.

You may have never realized what a complicated undertaking this is for a young child to master!

right for the family. No matter what the advertisements would lead you to believe, toilet training is not a one-day event; it is a process that can take many weeks, or even months, from start to finish. Parents must be actively involved in reminding, coaching and helping their child every few hours, every day. They must also handle the cleaning up and clothes changing that must occur after the inevitable accidents. The entire training process can be frustrating for a parent who isn't prepared for the task, but it can be a pleasant one for a parent who knows what to expect and who is prepared for the journey.

The Quiz

The following quiz will help you assess whether you and your child are ready to begin potty training by giving you more insight into what indicators to look for.

Jot down the letter codes for each of your answers. Then consult the formula to determine scoring. Your score will direct you to the best chapter in this book to help you start your potty training journey.

1. My toddler tells me when he's got a wet or messy nappy:
    a. Are you kidding? He doesn't notice, couldn't care less, or wears those low-slung nappies proudly. (Either that, or I'm the one too busy to notice!)
    b. He seems to know that it's wet or messy but isn't in a hurry to get changed.
    c. Some days he couldn't care less, but other days he wants the nappy off as soon as possible.

    d. Always. He doesn't like wearing a wet or messy nappy!

2. When my toddler is having a bowel movement, she:
   a. Gives no sign. I only know it when I smell it!
   b. Sometimes makes it obvious; other times she's too distracted to notice.
   c. Stops everything and concentrates. (She may even go off to a private corner.)

3. My toddler's bowel movements:
   a. Are unpredictable. They can happen at any time and can catch me by surprise.
   b. Aren't always predictable in timing, but we always know when one is approaching by her actions or signs.
   c. Are regular and predictable. They happen about the same time every day.

4. My toddler understands the meaning of the words *wet, dry, clean, dirty, wash, sit* and *go*:
   a. No, he does not understand the meaning of these words.
   b. Sometimes he seems to understand the meaning of these words.
   c. Yes, he clearly understands the meaning of these words.
   d. He understands not only these words but more complex ideas as well, such as where to put his wet clothes or how to clean up a spill.

5. If I ask my toddler to put a toy in the toy box:
   a. He ends up playing with the toy and never makes it to the toy box.
   b. Sometimes he makes it to the toy box; other times he gets distracted.

    c. He immediately and proudly puts the toy in the toy box.

    d. I don't even have to ask. He knows where his toys belong, and he often puts them away without prompting. (Well, OK, not always, but on occasion!)

6. When my toddler tries to dress herself, she:

    a. Has no clue where anything goes or how to put it on.

    b. Knows where things belong but just can't get the clothes to cooperate.

    c. Can manage to put on easy clothes, such as elastic-waist trousers, with some help.

    d. Can put on her trousers, shirt and socks all by herself. (She probably can't manage buttons or poppers just yet.)

7. When I read a book to my child, he:

    a. Doesn't seem to know I'm reading—he just keeps on playing.

    b. Sits still for a page or two.

    c. Sometimes sits to listen and sometimes wanders off. When he stays to listen, he takes an interest in the pictures.

    d. Sits and listens to one or two short books.

    e. Sits still and listens to books for as long as I'm willing to read!

8. My child loves to imitate others. If she sees me, siblings, older friends or cousins doing something, she wants to try to do it, too.

    a. I haven't noticed this.

    b. She imitates mainly when prodded, such as when we say, "Wave bye-bye!"

    c. Yes, I'm starting to see some imitation, every once
      in a while.

    d. All the time! She's like a little impersonator!

9. When a family member is using the toilet and my
   toddler is nearby, he:

    a. Is busy playing and doesn't notice.

    b. Sometimes seems interested but other times
      ignores it.

    c. Has been interested and curious. (Sometimes
      more than I'd like!)

    d. Has demonstrated an understanding of what the
      toilet is for.

10. I change my toddler's nappy:

    a. Frequently, every hour or two.

    b. It varies. Sometimes she stays dry longer than
      other times.

    c. Wow! I never realized it, but she consistently
      stays dry for two or more hours.

11. My toddler is:

    a. Younger than fifteen months.

    b. Between fifteen months and twenty months.

    c. Between twenty months and twenty-four months.

    d. Between twenty-four months and thirty months.

    e. Older than thirty months.

12. When my toddler is in the bathroom and I flush the
   toilet, she:

    a. Gets scared or worried.

    b. Doesn't ever notice.

    c. Is sometimes interested in the flushing and has
      even done it herself (or she tries).

    d. Seems to accept or understand that a person
      flushes after using the toilet.

13. This is how I would describe my toddler's communication skills:
    a. She is just starting to communicate her needs and can only say or sign a few basic words.
    b. She can get her essential needs across to us with words or sign language.
    c. She has a good vocabulary consisting of monosyllabic words and can use simple sentences as well.
    d. Are you kidding? She never *stops* talking!
14. This is how I feel about changing nappies:
    a. I enjoy that one-on-one time with my toddler or at least I think I'd prefer changing nappies over running him to the potty every hour.
    b. I don't mind. I never really think about it.
    c. I'd welcome a move out of nappies.
    d. I've had enough of nappies! Bring on the pants!
15. This is how I feel about potty training my child right now:
    a. Either I'm not even thinking about it yet, I don't think my child is ready, or I don't have the time or energy to train her right now.
    b. I'm OK with it. I know it's part of the parenting process.
    c. I think my child is ready, so I'm ready, too.
    d. I'm excited! I see it as a fun time of growth for my child.
16. My toddler often wants to do things "all by myself", such as putting on his socks, climbing into his car seat, or pouring his juice:
    a. Never. He's happy for me to take care of him.
    b. I'm just starting to see some of this independence emerging.

    c. He frequently demonstrates independence in some areas.

    d. Oh, yeah, that's my baby: Mr. Independent! or Miss Do It Myself!

17. When my toddler wants to put on his socks, climb into his car seat, or pour his juice, my response is to:

    a. Do it for him. He can't do it yet, even though he wants to.

    b. Depends on the day and the task: sometimes I'm patient, sometimes I'm not.

    c. Encourage him to try, if we have time.

    d. Usually let him do it, no matter how long it takes.

18. Our family right now:

    a. Is going through a stressful time, but our family situation isn't expected to change in the next year or more.

    b. Is unusually busy but happy!

    c. Is functioning normally. (Considering that with kids in the house, "normal" is a moving target!)

    d. Is happy lately. It's been calm and peaceful around here.

    e. Is going through a stressful time, but it's temporary—we should be back to normal in a month or two.

19. Over the next two months, this is what I expect to be going on in our household:

    a. Life will be disrupted for a major reason (for example, we'll be taking a long trip, we'll be moving, we're redecorating, we're getting married, we'll be having another baby, or we're expecting a houseful of company for an extended visit). We don't mind doing some pre-potty training but should probably wait a while for the active lessons.

b. We'll be dealing with some disruptions. Nevertheless, we don't mind starting the active training process now, even if it means dealing with a setback afterward.

c. We'll be home most of the time, but we'll have a few brief and minor disruptions—for example, having company, celebrating Christmas, visiting away from home for a day, and so on.

d. Our routine will be pretty normal. (Even if "normal" is busy.)

e. We'll have extra time on our hands and be home without the usual disruptions—for example, at home on holiday or in between assignments.

f. Life will be disrupted for a major reason, and we do not want to get things started and have to deal with a setback that forces us to start over again later.

20. I am considering potty training because:

a. Someone else advised me to start, or I read or heard something that led me to believe I should start potty training.

b. I think that my child is the right age for potty training.

c. I have a gut feeling that my child is ready.

d. Either we have a nursery or other deadline or my child is interested and asked to use the toilet more than once.

e. I'd have to pick more than one of the preceding answers!

f. I'm not even considering potty training yet—I'm just curious about what's to come.

21. If my results on this quiz say my child *is not ready* to start potty training now:
    a. I'll agree 100 per cent.
    b. I kind of suspected as much.
    c. I'll take the quiz again and change some of my answers.
    d. I'll think this quiz was clever but totally wrong.
22. If my results on this quiz say my child *is ready* to start potty training now:
    a. I'll think this quiz was wrong.
    b. I'll take the quiz again and rethink some of my answers.
    c. I suspected as much.
    d. I'll agree 100 per cent.

Total the number of responses for each letter, multiply this number by the value shown, and then add up the total sum for each letter to get a total score.

a. _____ × 0 = _____
b. _____ × 1 = _____
c. _____ × 2 = _____
d. _____ × 3 = _____
e. _____ × 5 = _____
f. _____ × −5 = _____

TOTAL SCORE = _____

0 to 15: *Wait.*

Your little one doesn't seem to be ready for this big step just yet. Maybe you're not ready either. So if it's possible, wait a few months and then take this quiz again. Rushing a child through the toilet training process before both parties are ready is likely to result in tears

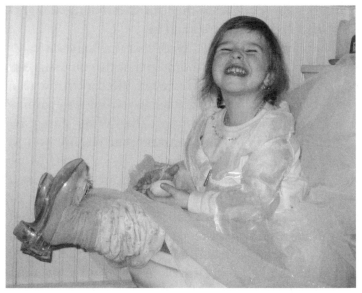

Sedona, two years old

and frustration—for both of you. Starting too soon could actually prolong the experience and make it unpleasant. On the other hand, if you wait until your little one is more receptive and physically able, the process will be much easier.

If you're expecting any major disruption to family life in the coming weeks, do yourselves a favour and hold off until things settle down a bit. It's difficult for a toddler to begin potty training only to have the process derailed before the learning is completed. Having to restart the potty training process all over again once things settle back to normal can be frustrating for parents, too. And fitting in potty training because of an imagined rule when you're already stressed to the maximum just makes it another chore added to the list instead of the delightful shared experience it should be.

What if your score says "Wait" but you honestly can't wait? Oh, if only it were so simple that this quiz suggests you wait and so you do! However, life can throw us a few curved balls, particularly when it comes to parenting. Even if you've ended up in the "Wait" category, you may have important reasons that require you to begin potty training nonetheless. Have heart! More than half of the children in the world are toilet trained around their first birthday—mainly out of necessity or because of cultural practices. So this shows you that early potty training before readiness *can* be done. It will just require an extra dose of humour, additional patience, more parental involvement, and a bit more planning.

No matter what your goals or plans, if you have scored in the "Wait" category, it's a good time to read through this book and get yourself acquainted with the process. It's a great time to review the pre-potty training ideas that begin on page 39 and introduce some of these into your daily routine with your child.

16 to 24: *Time for pre-potty training—get ready!*

Don't throw out those nappies just yet! Your child probably isn't ready to begin learning to use the potty in earnest, but you can take many helpful steps that will prepare your toddler for the near future. You'll find lots of ideas in Chapter 3.

You may want to read through the actual potty training steps so that you're more apt to identify when your child is ready for that next step and so that you'll be more prepared when that opportune time comes.

25 to 39: *You can make a choice: either begin to set things up with pre-potty training or jump right into toilet training.*

Your child is likely to be showing many of the signs of readiness for potty training. There may be a few things that don't quite click yet. Or possibly something's going on in your home that could be disruptive to the potty training process.

As with so many aspects of parenting, there is no one right answer. There really isn't only one exactly right time to potty train. There are many variables involved in making this decision, and you and your child can easily go either way.

Examine your child's needs, personality and readiness. Contemplate your own readiness. Look at your calendar. Read through the chapters on pre-potty training and potty training, and then do what feels right to you.

No matter what direction you choose—either to start slowly with pre-potty training or jump right in to active potty training—as long as you have a positive attitude and use a relaxed, planned approach, your child will likely follow your lead and joyfully embrace this new adventure.

40 to 80: *How exciting! Your toddler is clearly ready for potty training!*

Everything is lined up in your favour for a pleasant toilet training experience. Time to start using the potty!

Even though all the pieces appear to be in line, it's a good idea to begin by looking over the ideas for pre-potty training (see Chapter 3). These will set the stage for a positive experience. You may find that you are already doing many of these things, and that's good! Once you feel confident and prepared, move on to Chapter 4. This chapter will lead you through the process step-by-step to help you achieve a pleasant and successful potty training experience.

3

Pre-Potty Training: Getting Ready!

When children learn a new skill, they rarely learn it all at once. Typically, they learn in manageable pieces, a little at a time. Think about how your child learned to run. The process began way back when he was an infant and learned to hold up his head and shoulders and to control his body. He progressed to sitting, then to crawling, and on to walking while you held his hands. Soon he was cruising the furniture. After a time, he took those first shaky steps, and once those were mastered, he began to run. This natural sequence of events took anywhere from ten to twenty months of time.

In the same way that you patiently and methodically helped your child learn to run, you can encourage him to learn about the many details involved in toilet training. In the months before you actively begin potty training, you can do many things that set your child up for smooth sailing when the time is right.

Identify the Act

Every time you change your child's nappy, you have an opportunity to teach a little bit about elimination.

Making casual comments about elimination is a great way to teach. You might say, "You've made a poo-poo in your nappy. It came out of your bottom." Or, "Your nappy is wet because you weed. Mummy wees in the potty."

A few brief explanations over time are helpful. You can explain that the wetness is wee-wee and the brown stuff is poo-poo. Tell her that they're leftovers that her body doesn't need. Explain that a clean, dry nappy is much nicer to wear.

Help your toddler recognize what's happening when you notice that she's wetting or filling her nappy: "You're doing a poo-poo. When you get bigger, you'll do that in the potty."

If you haven't already, let her watch you empty the contents of her nappy into the toilet, and let her do the flushing. If you get her involved at an early age, she'll likely not develop any fears of flushing that sometimes crop up during potty training.

Lucky for you if you catch her tinkling in the bath or if you feel that sudden warmth in her nappy against you while carrying her. At these times you can point out what she's doing and let her know that in time she'll learn to do it in the potty.

Keep It Natural

Babies and toddlers accept the things that happen in their nappy as normal and natural. It isn't until siblings, peers and, yes, even adults teach them there's something disgusting or funny about these processes that they think otherwise. Try to let your child keep this innocent viewpoint about elimination. This can help

Isabella, three years old

toilet training to be a more positive experience devoid of any embarrassment or shame.

Don't attach negative value to wet or messy nappies. (That is, avoid words like *bad, icky, stinky* or *pee-ewww*.) Try not to make a big production about the smell or texture, and do your best to control big brothers and sisters on this one!

Your toddler may still see his excretions as part of himself. (Many demonstrate this concept by waving bye-bye before they flush the toilet!) Though it's perfectly fine and natural if he does this, it's best if *you* don't personalize his stool, as you might inadvertently send the message that it is indeed part of his body.

Teaching the Vocabulary

During your everyday events, teach your toddler the words and meanings for toilet-related items such as body parts, urination, bowel movements and toilet tasks. When the time comes for actual potty training, there is so much to learn, so it will be helpful if she already is comfortable with the basic information.

Lots of words that are used during potty training aren't directly toilet related but will be important concepts for your child to understand. Descriptive words that you will use during the process are those like *wet, dry, wash, flush* and *toilet paper*.

Teach your child the concept of opposites and specific ideas that will provide a foundation for toilet training. Wet/dry, on/off, messy/clean, up/down, stop/go, now/later—these are all concepts that will be a part of the potty training routine.

It's common for parents to use a combination of phrases and terms during the potty process, but doing so can confuse a new trainee. If one day you ask him if he has to "go on the potty" but the next day you take him "to the toilet" and later ask him if he has to "tinkle", he may not follow your train of thought. It's best if you decide on your vocabulary terms and stick to them during the learning process.

Choose Your Potty Words!

Certain words are common in specific geographic areas, and some are more widely used than others. If you listen in at nursery, the park, or out shopping, you'll soon know what words are most often used.

Here are some of the words most commonly used by families with young children:

Term	Family Words
toilet	toilet, potty, privy, loo
urination	pee, pee-pee, go pee-pee, tinkle, wee-wee, go number one, wee, wees, go to the bathroom, go to the toilet, use the potty, go (as in, "Do you have to go?")
bowel movement	poop, poopie, poo-poo, poos, caca, BM, go poo-poo, number two, use the potty, go to the bathroom, push out a poo
vulva (what you can see) and vagina (the canal inside)	vulva, vagina, privates, bottom, girl parts, front bottom, bits, tina, gina gina, fanny*
penis	penis, privates, pee-pee, willy
buttocks/rectum	bottom, bum, tush, tushy, cheeks, behind, rear, rear end
flatulence	gas, passing gas, passing wind, fart*, toot, breaking wind, blow off, stinker, parp/trumpet

*Considered a rude term for children in some families but normal in others.

Actual scientific or technical terms sound odd when used with a child. Can you imagine yourself asking your little one, "Do you have pressure in your rectum indicating that you must defecate?" Instead, decide on words that you would be comfortable having your child use. Use whatever words with which your family is most comfortable and familiar; keep in mind that these words will most likely be called out by your toddler in a public place, so it's safer to stick to socially acceptable language. (See the list of common potty words on page 43.)

The Value of Demonstrations

It can be helpful to let your child watch you or her siblings use the toilet. It's not necessary to have her watch every detail; it's often enough to have her see you sit on the toilet while you explain what you are doing. Tell her that when she gets bigger, she'll put her wee-wee and poo-poo in the toilet, too, instead of in her nappy.

If your child has older siblings, cousins or friends, tell her that they used nappies when they were her age, but now they use the toilet. If they are open to company in the toilet, let your little one get a glimpse of a sibling or peer using the potty. Let her know that when she gets a little bigger, she'll make that change, too.

Not every parent is willing to have little eyes watching while they use the toilet, and it's not necessary for you to do this. If you prefer your privacy, then teach your child to respect a closed bathroom door. Keep in mind that as your child masters her own toileting, she is likely to follow in your footsteps and desire her own privacy as well. Set up the bathroom so that it's safe and

Hannah, two years old

manageable for her, and keep an ear open when she is alone in the bathroom.

When Should You Buy a Potty?

Some parents like to wait to purchase a potty until active training begins, because the appearance of a brand-new object usually causes a spike in interest. Others like to get a potty and put it in the bathroom a few months ahead of time to get a child accustomed to it. If you elect to get a potty before training begins, you may want to present it to your child with an enthusiastic voice and let her sit on it. Allow her to take the pieces apart and open and shut the lid, if it has one.

When you bring this new item home, talk to your child about its purpose. You can even invite your child to sit on her potty when you use the big toilet. You can leave it in the bathroom for a few weeks or more to let your child get used to the idea before the teaching process even begins.

If you decide to wait until training commences, make sure that you purchase the potty and take it out of the box and put it together before presenting it to your child. (Potty and potty options are compared for you in Chapter 4.)

Learning to Follow Directions

When you start active potty training, your child will need to know how to follow your directions. "Come into the bathroom." "Pull down your trousers." "Sit on the potty." The list of instructions will be long.

Start now by giving your child simple directions and helping him follow them. Ask him to put a toy in the toy box. Ask her to put the cup in the sink.

At first you'll need to do a lot of prompting and reminding. You may even have to go with her to help her carry out your request. Over time, she'll begin to do things on her own. When she does, praise her and reward her with hugs and kisses. Let her know you're proud of her for being such a big girl.

Helping your child to understand and follow directions and to feel good about doing so are important steps necessary for successful toilet training.

Promote Your Child's Independence

Now is the time to encourage your child to do things on her own—for example, put on her socks, pull up her trousers, take off her jacket, carry a plate to the table, and climb into her car seat. All of these tasks nurture the feeling of independence that will be necessary for potty mastery.

As your child masters each task, her level of confidence will grow. The more that she can do, the more she will be willing to try. Each success builds on previous successes, and your child will see herself as someone who can try new things and be good at doing them. This attitude will be especially helpful when the time comes to introduce potty training.

Read to Your Child

Most children enjoy books and love to be read to. Many great children's books, written precisely for toddlers, are available on the subject of potty training. Try to balance those books that have photographs of real children with books that use colourful pictures of animals and pretend creatures learning how to use the toilet.

Reading these books in advance of training will help your child become familiar with the idea in a fun, non-threatening way with no expectations attached. You can also use these same books as potty-time reading when training begins. (See "Read About the Potty" in Chapter 5.)

Moving on from Pre-Potty Training to Active Toilet Training

Take some time to become comfortable with these pre-potty training ideas and include the ones that appeal to you in your daily routine. You can retake the readiness quiz (see Chapter 2) from time to time to help you decide when you're ready to make the move to active potty training.

4

It's Potty Time! Setting Up

You've decided that the time is here. Your child is ready. You're ready. So what's next?

First, make sure your attitude and expectations are in the right place. You should be feeling relaxed and positive. You should also understand that the learning process can take as long as six months or more, so let go of any hope you might have to toilet train your toddler in only a day. Just like learning how to walk, talk, or drink from a cup, learning to use the toilet can, and should, be a gradual, pleasant experience for both of you.

Before you even place a potty in the bathroom, though, it's time to set up your supplies and do a little planning.

Deciding on Your Potty Training Approach

There isn't just one right way to potty train a child. There are many different approaches that can lead you to success. As you make decisions about how to embark upon this grand endeavour, take a few things into consideration:

- **What is your child's learning style?** How has she learned other new skills? Does she observe and absorb before she tackles something? Or does she dive right in and work her way through it? Is she a thoughtful listener or a hands-on doer?
- **What things do you do that most encourage her to try something new?** What actions bring the best results? Is your enthusiasm enough to get your child to attempt something new? Or do you need to convince and persuade her before she'll give it a try? Will she do anything her older sibling or cousin does?
- **What is your teaching style?** Do you explain verbally before you show? Do you show step-by-step with commentary? Do you silently demonstrate? Do you set things up and let your child figure out what's happening on his own?
- **How much time do you have?** Are you home all day with your child or home only part of the day? Will you have an uninterrupted chunk of time to get started, followed by snippets of time every day afterward? Or will you be fitting training into bits of time in your already busy day?
- **What are your goals?** What do you think would be easier for you: changing nappies or assisting your child on the potty? Would you rather focus intently on potty training for a couple of weeks and move things along? Or are you content to coach and teach while you let your child set the pace, mastering one step at a time?
- **Who will be the teachers?** Will you potty train on your own? Or will more than one person be involved in the training?

All of these issues will affect the toilet training experience. Taking some time to consider these points will help you plan the best approach for you, your child and the rest of your family, too.

The Magic Two

Whether you are using elimination communication with a three-month-old, pre-training an eighteen-month-old, or introducing a brand-new concept to a three-year-old, there are two magic factors that will affect the process more than anything else.

These two magic factors will set the pace for potty training. These can make the toilet training journey a stressful, unpleasant event, or they can ensure that it is a pleasant, successful process.

These two factors can make your child miserable, or they can make him happy. They can make any approach a disappointing disaster, or they can make almost any toilet training method work beautifully.

What are these Magic Two? The teacher's attitude and the teacher's level of patience.

Allow me to repeat that idea for you, just to be certain you grasp this critical concept. The two magic factors that will set the pace for potty training are your attitude and your patience.

You'll note that I didn't mention anything about the student! That's because children learn things from their parents and other people in their life—that's what they do. And children are like little sponges. Children are always watching others, especially the adults in their lives. They pick up cues from others about how they should respond in various situations; no matter if it's the first time on a horse, the first taste of a melon, or the first sit on a potty, your child will be learning from you.

So regardless of where your child is in the readiness department, and no matter what approach you decide to take, make sure that your Magic Two are in the right place before you begin.

The Two Magic Indicators for Toilet Training Success

- The teacher's positive and supportive attitude.
- The teacher's kind and understanding patience.

Supplies You'll Need

It's best to have everything you need on hand before starting the potty training process. The following information will help you create your own shopping list for supplies.

A Potty or Adapter Seat

A normal adult toilet doesn't fit a child very well. It's hard to climb up to it, and then a child has to balance and hold himself up while seated, making elimination more difficult. The hole is usually large enough for a child to fall through, into the water, which can be a frightening experience. A better choice for a new trainee is a child-sized potty or an adapter seat insert accompanied by a sturdy footstool.

There are many, many different types available, so shop around. A child-sized chair or seat insert is important to help bring the toilet down to your child's size and make it friendly, safe and manageable. Nearly any

Bailey, two years old

type will work, and the choice is yours. (See the chart that follows for a comparison.)

Some potty seats come with a high, removable splash guard created to prevent a new trainee from splattering the bathroom. While the intention for these is good and they can serve the purpose, splash guards also present an injury hazard. Many children lose their balance

Comparing the Potty Choices

Freestanding Potty

Pros
- It is small in size, easy to use and nonthreatening.
- It is designed specifically for a child's small body.
- It allows the child to plant his feet on the floor.
- It comes in bright colours and child-friendly designs.
- It is portable—can be moved from room to room or taken on trips.
- It promotes independence—can be used by a child on his own.

Cons
- The bowl must be cleaned out after each use.
- The child will have to transition to a regular toilet later.
- The child may still need a toilet seat insert when moving up to the big toilet.
- When you are away from home, you must bring the potty or your child must adjust to the differences in equipment.
- Portability can make it too much like a toy (leaving it open to misuse): a toy box? a hat?
- You must purchase one for each bathroom or move it from one bathroom to another.

Toilet Seat Insert (Adapter/Potty)

Pros
- The child doesn't have to adjust from a child seat to an adult toilet.

- You will not have a potty on your bathroom floor.
- There is no potty bowl to clean out.

Cons

- It is not child-sized.
- The child must use a stool or have an adult's help to climb up.
- The child's feet will dangle, so a footstool (where the child can place her feet) is necessary.
- Adults must contend with the insert when they use the toilet.
- The child must be supervised by an adult throughout all uses.
- You must purchase one for each bathroom or move it from one bathroom to another.

Adult Toilet Seat

Pros

- There is no learning adjustment from seat to seat.
- The child can use any toilet once he learns to use the one at home.

Cons

- It is not as enticing to a child as a colourful child's potty chair.
- It is oversized for a child, which can be intimidating.
- The child might fall off the seat or into the water.
- The child will need a footstool to plant feet.
- The child must be supervised by an adult throughout all uses.

(continued)

Comparing the Potty Choices, *continued*

Potty Buying Checklist
◇ The seat size matches the child's body size.
◇ The splash guard is low, padded or removable.
◇ The base is stable and sturdy.
◇ The bowl is easy to remove for cleaning.
◇ The seat is comfortable, perhaps cushioned.
◇ It is portable for moving from room to room or for travel.
◇ It has an appealing design.
◇ It has good functionality.

climbing over the guard and fall or might get bruised in a very delicate area when climbing on or off the potty. Either of these situations can cause a fear of the potty and create a major setback. Better to teach your little boy to hold his penis down to wee and your little girl to relax and lean forward a bit, instead of backward, which will prevent any splashing.

If you opt to use an insert that fits into the regular toilet, you'll need to get one to fit your toilet seat, which may be round or elongated. You will also need a stool. This serves two purposes: to help your child climb up to the seat and to use as a platform for his feet. It is much harder to control the sphincter muscles when feet are dangling in the air.

If your child spends time in two different homes, or if the bathrooms in your home are far apart from each other, buy several of the same potty to keep things easy and consistent.

Consider your child's personality in advance of purchasing a potty for him. Do you think he'll be more accepting of the potty if he goes with you to the shop to pick it out? If so, go ahead and shop together. Take one out of the box and let him sit on it in the shop. Or perhaps your child would like it better if you wrapped one up in colourful wrapping paper and presented it to him with a flourish. Either choice is fine.

A Portable Potty

No matter what kind of toilet arrangement you have at home, it's likely that your child will be facing a different situation when she's away. It's often helpful to purchase a seat adjuster that you can keep in your purse or nappy bag. This is a folding insert that you can use when you're away from home. It adapts bigger toilets to your child's size and makes them a little more familiar, which is important for new trainees who are comfortable with a little potty at home but might be overwhelmed or frightened by a big toilet in a public place.

It's a good idea to practise using this portable adjuster at home a few times before you go out. Otherwise it's just as unfamiliar as the strange toilet you are placing it upon.

Training Pants

Get a supply of a dozen or more cotton training pants or a couple of boxes of disposable pull-ups. These will herald the new stage of development for your child and be a clear signal that something new has begun.

Thick, absorbent training pants (rather than regular underwear) are great for new trainees. They will absorb most or all of your child's accidents (which will be many at first) and protect your floors and furniture.

Disposable pull-ups, which contain accidents, are a popular choice for new trainees. Be aware, however, that the disposables can backfire (so to speak). Because they may feel like nappies to your child, your child may treat them as such. Look into one of the new varieties that are a little less unwieldy and have a get-wet liner that allows your child to feel the moisture, which will help him to identify, and hopefully avoid, that wet feeling.

Children can move on to less bulky and more attractive underwear once they start to have some success. In addition, the switch from training pants to big girl or big boy pants can be motivating and will be something special your child can look forward to.

Tricks and Treats

Lots of interesting accessories are available for potty training: musical potty chairs, bull's-eye targets, toddler-sized urinals, dissolving floaters, dolls that wet, and prize charts are some examples. None of these are necessary, but lots of them are fun, and some can motivate your child and move the process happily along.

Choose your tricks thoughtfully, though, because some can be more of a distraction than a help. Several parents told me of using musical potties and having their children jump up midstream to see what was going on behind them!

If something catches your eye and you think it will make the process more fun for your child, go ahead and try it.

Decide Where to Put the Potty

If you are using a potty instead of an insert, you can place it wherever you'd like. Many families put the potty in the bathroom right next to the big toilet. The advantage to this is that your child gets used to the location, and it makes for easy dumping and cleaning. It also helps a child connect the potty with the action, because other members of the family use the toilet in the same room.

The disadvantage to keeping your child's potty near the toilet is that if your bathroom is far away from the places in your home where your child spends his time, then you may have a number of accidents at first while he's on the way to the bathroom. This will pass, however, as your child gets used to reading his body signals.

Some families choose to keep the potty in the room where the child spends his time. During the day it can be kept in the kitchen. If you do this, it's a good idea to create a little potty nook or corner to allow a child some privacy and to reinforce the idea that this isn't a public event. During the bedtime routine and overnight, the potty can be kept in the bedroom for easy access, if you'd like. The advantage to a movable potty is that your child is more likely to get to the pot in time. The disadvantage is that at some point you'll need to transfer your child's toileting to the bathroom,

Kailee, three and a half years old

but most children make this change easily once they are toilet trained.

Tips for Toilet Training

Once you've decided on how you'll approach potty training with your child and gathered all your supplies, it's almost time to actively begin the process. Following are a few things to consider as you move forward.

> ⭐ **Mother-Speak**
>
> "It is really convenient to carry the potty from room to room. If I bring the potty to Thomas, it's usually to the place both boys are playing, so I don't have to worry about the baby running off unsupervised or becoming distracting to Thomas. Having the potty in the kitchen is especially convenient if Damon is in the high chair and Thomas needs to do a wee."
>
> **—Suzanne, mother of two-year-old Thomas and eleven-month-old Damon**

Remember the Magic Two!

The teacher's positive attitude and kind patience will set the pace for the toilet training journey. Take a deep breath, relax, and enjoy the experience with your little one.

Take It Slowly

The Murphy's rule of potty training seems to be "The more you rush, the longer it will take." Even if a nursery or other deadline looms, don't rush the process with too much intensity and pressure. Being more relaxed will help your child learn more easily and will make this less stressful for you, too.

If you feel peaceful about the process, it's likely your child will as well. Ironically, the less you push, the more quickly the results will occur.

Grandfather-Speak

"All I hear around the house is talk about the potty training. I think everyone should relax. A year from now they won't even remember all the fuss and hullabaloo."

—Joseph, father of six and grandfather of four,
including thirty-two-month-old Jesse

Dress for Success

It's challenging enough for a toddler to make it to the toilet in time without adding the complication of poppers, zips, and buttons. Many a trainee has made it to the bathroom only to have an accident standing in front of the toilet, attempting to undress. For the next few months and probably even longer, your child should, whenever possible, avoid wearing trousers with buttons, poppers, belts, or zips and shirts that hang lower than the waist. Make sure that your child can remove her clothing easily and quickly. In the case of dresses, make sure they are short enough to be moved entirely out of the way.

The best clothing for a new potty trainee is a T-shirt and shorts or trousers with an elastic waistband. Make sure these are somewhat loose fitting so that your child can easily get them up and down.

At the beginning of training, you may want to have your child actually remove his trousers and underwear when he uses the potty, because there are a lot of new things to think about and having a wad of material around his ankles can be distracting and partially lowered trousers can become splattered. If you do ask him to remove his trousers, feel free to help him take his clothes off and put them back on, even if he can do it himself. Having to dress and undress ten times a day can get old fast for an active toddler and may lead to disinterest in using the potty at all. Don't worry, though—he'll master this part of the process in no time.

Less Is Best

If you're lucky enough to begin training in warm weather, or if you can turn the heat up in your home during training, keep your toddler in just training pants for a week or so. Children often resist dealing with all the up and down and on and off required during training, as it takes so much time and effort given their limited abilities. So the less clothing to deal with, the better!

Some parents let their children roam naked during training, but it's not for everyone. Think about it before you introduce the idea to your little one, because she is likely to love the freedom and may surprise you by doing a little more of it than you planned. You may want to consider your family's approach to nudity. How are things handled during bathtime? How do you respond if your child walks in as you are dressing? If your family culture is one of modesty and you suddenly let your child roam the house naked, it may send her some confusing mixed messages.

On the other hand, some families are more relaxed about the body's natural state. Children, siblings and parents bathe together, toddlers play in the bathroom as Mummy showers and dresses, and little boys potty

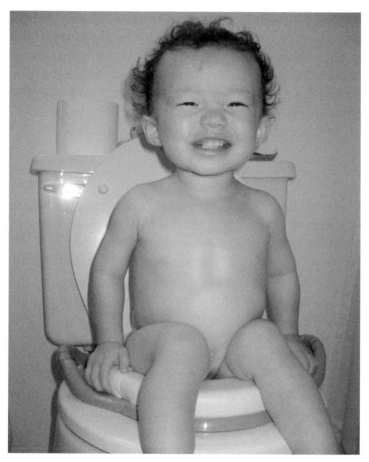

Jude, twenty-two months old

train while weeing alongside Daddy. If this describes your family, then you might find a little extra nudie time can help your child become more in tune with her body's elimination process.

One other thing to think about here is that when using the naked approach, all those early accidents (and there are many) will be unhindered by clothing and land unprotected wherever your child may be, and it won't be her fault or anything you can prevent. If you have carpeting or furniture that could be ruined by accidents, you might take the training out to the garden or opt to go the nearly naked approach instead and pop a pair of training pants on your little one.

Training Pants or Disposables?

Once your child has the general idea and has started having daily success on the potty, you may want to switch from nappies or disposable pull-ups to cloth training pants to move things along even quicker.

The drawback to thickly padded disposable nappies or super-absorbent training pants is that they disguise wetness so much that your child probably isn't bothered by it, whereas cotton training pants, or disposables with a stay-wet liner, signal wetness immediately and aren't very comfortable to wear when wet or messy. This will help your child become more aware of what's happening down there.

Also, remember to keep your child's pants a bit loose so your little one can pull them up and down easily. Training pants or pull-ups should be a size bigger than necessary. You want them to be manageable for your child, without being so big that they droop.

Make the Bathroom Child-Friendly

Can your toddler easily open the door and turn on the light? Reach the toilet paper? Get up to the sink? If she has a difficult time getting to and using her potty, she will be less interested in using it routinely. Also, if she counts on you to do everything for her, you'll be missing out on a wonderful aspect of potty training: encouraging your child's independence.

Many young children are wary of empty rooms, and many fear the dark. There's nothing scarier than the cavern of a dark bathroom at the end of an empty hallway. During the training months, and possibly even for a long time after training, accept that you will either have to accompany your child each time or keep the hallway and bathroom well lit to chase away any unwanted shadows.

Pottying Away from Home

New trainees may be just getting comfortable with the potty routine at home but are unlikely to have the same success in public places or while driving from place to place. It can be frustrating for a parent to have to deal with repeated accidents in the car or while away from home. There are a number of ways to handle being away from home with a child in training.

You can simply decide to keep your child in nappies or pull-ups when away from home. Most children easily adapt to the idea that there is a switch into nappies or pull-ups when you leave the house. Create a routine: the child goes on the potty and puts on pull-ups before you leave the house and then changes back into training pants or underwear when you return home.

Other options here are to put your child's nappy or pull-ups over his training pants or use a waterproof nappy cover over his training pants. He may feel happier if he can keep his big boy pants on, yet he'll feel the wetness if he has an accident. It's kind of a midstep that can keep you relaxed in the car while helping him see that he is growing up.

If you'd prefer not to put your child into nappies when you leave your home, make sure that you are prepared to handle on-the-road potty calls and potty accidents. Bring along a portable potty for use in the car and a folding seat adapter for use in bathrooms. Cover the car seat with plastic, and for cleanup, bring along wet wipes, plastic bags and paper towels. Be prepared with a complete change of clothing, right down to socks and shoes.

And remember to bring your patience and good humour, too. There *will* be accidents, so accept them, clean them up, change your child's clothing, and move on.

Naps and Bedtime

Many children will stay in night-time nappies for a year or longer after daytime success. Night-time dryness is achieved only when a child's biology supports this—you can't rush it, so don't even try. (Occasional bed-wetting is considered normal until about age seven.)

Maintain a routine of putting nappies or disposable pull-ups on your child for naps or bedtime. As soon as he is awake, remove these and have him use the potty, as most children will eliminate very soon after waking up. Switch your child out of night-time nappies when the morning nappy is consistently dry. (For more information, read Chapter 5.)

Have Realistic Expectations

Learning to master toileting is a big job for a little person. Mastery will come in fits and bursts. Some days will be more successful than others. On days when the home is peaceful and the daily routine is in place, your child will likely have more success.

Learn to Read Your Child's Body Signals So That You Can Help Her Get to the Toilet on Time

Following are some common signals that a bowel movement is imminent:

- passing wind
- squatting
- touching nappy
- tense facial expression
- grunting
- stopping active play
- bending forward while holding tummy
- stomach ache
- timing (first thing in the morning or ten to thirty minutes after a full meal)

And here are some common signals of impending urination:

- squirming and wiggling (the potty dance)
- bouncing
- shifting from foot to foot
- rocking back and forth
- holding crotch
- sitting on heels
- crossing legs
- squeezing thighs together
- becoming still and motionless
- whimpering
- timing (first thing upon awakening in the morning or after a nap, one and a half to two hours since last wee, or twenty to forty-five minutes after drinking)

Mother-Speak

"I think the most important thing to keep in mind is that this is their accomplishment and milestone, not ours. It's important to be sensitive to their timeline. The more we support them in having their own success and their own accomplishment (with as little emotional attachment on our part as possible), the quicker the success and the more pleasant the experience for child and parents!"

—Natasha, mother of seventeen-month-old Jubal and five-year-old Max

When your child's daily routine is disrupted or when he's overtired, hungry or overstimulated, it's likely that he'll have more accidents and be more forgetful about what he's supposed to be doing.

Teaching your child how to use the toilet can seem to take for ever. Between dry runs and actual potty calls, you might find yourself taking him to the toilet up to a dozen times a day! That adds up to 84 separate visits to the bathroom over a week's time and some 360 visits in a month! (I know what you're thinking. If she would have told me that on page 1, I might have bought a box of nappies instead of this book.)

One way to keep perspective is to jot down the starting date of potty training and note another date three months in the future. Know that you'll be your little one's potty partner for at least those three months. Remember, on average it takes three to twelve months from the start of training until your child will be going to the bathroom independently.

5

A Menu of Potty Training Ideas

Every child is different, every parent is different, and every toilet training situation is entirely different; for those reasons, it's foolhardy to think that one exact method will work the same way with every family. Lots of people are misled into trying a plan that worked beautifully for someone else but that falls flat for them, because it doesn't mesh with their family's unique personality. Many of the basic principles of potty training will be common to all, but the variations on the process are vast. So take a little time to map out your plan before you get started or before you start again after a previously unsuccessful attempt at potty training.

This chapter provides you with many suggestions and ideas. So grab a pen or highlighter and read through these pages with your particular needs in mind, marking as you go. Then decide what exactly you'll be doing over the next few months.

Introduce the Potty

Sure, your child has been in the room when you've used the toilet. But chances are she's had no clue what

Kyleigh, sixteen months old

you were up to. She's also been eliminating in her nappy without giving it a thought for a long time. The idea of doing her business in the potty is almost certainly a brand-new concept—"You want me to do *what?! Where?!*" In some ways this will be like teaching your child a second language, so first things first. Tell her what's what.

Either take your child with you to select a potty or present one to her with a flourish. Give a brief lesson about what it's for, and then let her investigate this new contraption. Don't expect that she'll totally understand right off. It will take some time for her to really come to terms with how the potty will fit into her life.

If you haven't yet, start reading books to your child about other children who are learning to use the potty. I'd suggest that you read more than one or two, because some will make more sense to her than others, and she'll likely pick up an important point or two from each one. You might even want to write your own potty book, as discussed later in this chapter.

A few casual conversations about wee, poo and the potty are helpful, too. If you haven't before, start announcing your own trips to the toilet so your child can observe that you do this new thing, too.

Just Sitting There Is Success

When you first get started, just getting your busy toddler to *sit* on the potty for more than ten seconds is progress! Toddlers are full of energy, and during the learning time, your child may find it rather difficult to sit still long enough for something to actually happen. It might even be confusing to her, and she may be wondering, "What am I supposed to do here, anyway?" You may want to read, sing or talk with her while she is sitting so that she'll stay for longer than a moment or two. It won't be until she makes a few deposits into her potty or the toilet that she'll grasp exactly what you expect to happen when you have her sit there.

Praise your child for going through the actions of getting to the potty and sitting there, even if it's just for a moment. Let her know that you're proud of her attempts.

Don't Expect a Deposit Every Time!

At first, there will be lots and lots and *lots* of dry runs. Also, your trainee may wet or soil his nappy or training pants immediately after getting off the potty. This is because it's necessary to relax the muscles for elimination to occur. When potty training is a new event, your child will likely be excited, tense or distracted while sitting on the potty and will then relax as soon as a nappy or training pants are in place.

Remember, too, that your child has been used to eliminating while standing or even while on the go. Sitting still in one place to do his business is a new and unfamiliar concept and will take some getting used to.

Don't worry and don't scold if your child continues to make dry runs. He's not doing this to annoy you; he just can't quite read his body signals yet. Give him time. He will figure it out eventually.

At first, put a few pieces of toilet paper into the bottom of the potty, so that even a few drops of wee can be seen. If your child is using a toilet, put a few drops of blue food colouring into the water. Adding a bit of yellow urine will turn the water green, which will surely fascinate your child. You can also do this in a potty with a tablespoon or two of blue water.

Give Wiping and Toilet Paper Lessons

Children seem to have a hard time figuring out how much toilet paper to use. They either use too little, ending up with a messy hand, or use too much and can't control the wiping process. It will take a number of lessons before they get it right.

If you can use a tangible way to measure the paper, that works best. Common measuring tools are an arm's stretch length, counting squares, or unrolling the paper down to the floor.

Tristan, thirteen months old

If the toilet paper tube unrolls too fast and your child ends up with an excess amount, you can squeeze the roll a bit so that it flattens out and slows the unravelling.

Wiping after a bowel movement is a big job for little ones. It will take time for them to master this task, and they likely will not be doing it completely on their own until a year or more after completing their potty training. Be sure to teach your little girl to wipe from front to back to prevent infections.

Teach your child to wipe while sitting down. Children have a tendency to get up first and then wipe, which often leaves a smear along the toilet seat as they climb off.

You can start by doing the wiping and then let your child finish up. After a time, your child can start and you can finish up. Teach boys and girls to wipe until the paper is clean, which could take two or three fresh pieces of paper. A great idea is to use flushable wipes for the first wipe and toilet paper for the second.

Make It a Routine

It will take quite a while for your little one to remember to even ask to go. She'll have to learn how to read her body signals, understand what they mean, and act on them by stopping what she's doing and making the trip to the bathroom. An active toddler who is concentrating on play will often miss the signals or hope they'll go away so that she can finish her activity. She may also misjudge how long she has before her holding control stops. She may think she can put off going to the potty, but eventually her natural response will be to release, no matter where she is.

To help your child learn how this all works, have her sit on the potty at regular times at first—for example, when she first wakes up, after meals, before a bath,

Mother-Speak

"Anna does what we call the potty dance. She wiggles and shimmies while holding her crotch and shifting from foot to foot. It's entirely obvious that she has to go, but when you ask her if she has to use the toilet, she always says no!"

—**Julie, mother of three-year-old Anna**

before getting in the car, and before bed. In addition, watch your toddler closely, and anytime you think a visit to the potty might be timely, go ahead and take her.

Don't ask, "Do you need to go on the potty?" because the answer from a busy toddler will almost always be no (yet another case in which asking a yes-or-no question of a toddler is ill advised). Instead, make a positive suggestion, such as, "Let's go sit on the potty now." Positive works better than negative here—much better than saying, "Don't wait so long that you wee in your pants!" (Then she probably will.)

Offer Choices

Another way to encourage your child to use the potty is to offer interesting choices. Children love to be given choices and often will cooperate just because you've given them the freedom to choose. Here are a few great potty choices:

"Do you want to use the upstairs potty or the downstairs potty?"

"Do you want to walk to the potty or run to the potty?"

"Do you want to use the big toilet or your potty?"

"Shall we use the potty before snack or after snack?"

"What do you want to do first, get dressed or use the potty?"

"Do you want Mummy to come with you, or do you want to go all by yourself?"

Make It a Game

Why would your child want to interrupt his fun activities every two hours if going to the potty is a boring chore? If you can liven things up a bit, your child will be a more willing participant.

You might introduce a fun ritual for getting to the toilet. For example, call it the potty train. Announce its arrival with a loud "Choo! Choo!", and call "All aboard!" to your child, encouraging him to follow you. Chug around the room a bit and end up at the Potty Stop. If the train comes every few hours, and if it's a happy train, your child should willingly follow.

After a time, if the train loses its appeal, you can switch to an aeroplane and fly to the bathroom or become a circus parade or lions on the prowl or any other current imaginary favourite.

A variation on this game idea is to have a race to the bathroom. (Careful, though. Don't race if your child's been doing the potty dance—this might cause an accident!) You could also be spaceships and count down to launch time, or take advantage of your child's current favourite animal or cartoon character to create a fantasy journey to the bathroom.

Yes, you might find this all a little boring, and the choo-chooing and parading might be the last thing you feel like doing. But compared to begging an uninterested child to please, *please* sit on the potty, it's so much more effective!

Come with Me!

Most young children love to be with Mummy or Daddy no matter where you go, and they will happily join you in the bathroom when you have to go. If you've always been open about having your child in the bathroom with you, invite him to come with you when you go, and then suggest that he sit on his potty while you sit on yours. The two of you can talk or sing together while you sit side by side.

In some families, privacy is more closely guarded, and children don't accompany their parents into the bathroom or share the room when a parent is dressing. If this has been the way things work in your home, it's best not to change your behaviour now. There's no rule that says you must demonstrate toileting, and your child will learn how to use the potty even if he never sees you go.

Read About the Potty

There are lots and lots of books for children about potty training, because it is a popular toddler topic. But be forewarned! Many of them may be fun and entertaining for your child but aren't at all helpful when it comes to potty training. Some are vague and use words that don't match your own vocabulary. Some use pictures of potties that don't look anything like real potties. Some of these children's books are quite silly, and some demonstrate things you don't want your child to try, like wearing his potty on his head, turning his seat upside down, storing toys in the potty, or unrolling the whole roll of toilet paper. He may never have thought of these grand ideas until the book came along!

I strongly suggest that you read any children's potty books yourself before you read them to your child to make sure that they mesh with your potty training agenda. A list of suggested titles is on the next page.

Make a Custom Potty Book

The most perfect potty book is one about your very own child! You can create a personalized toilet training book for your child that will reinforce what you are teaching. It will likely become your child's favourite book.

Simply take photos of your child at every step of the potty process. The first photo should be of your child playing with toys, so you can explain that he must first identify the urge and stop what he's doing. The second will show your child's trip down the hallway, and the

Suggested Reading for Your Little Potty Learner

My Big Girl Potty and *My Big Boy Potty*
by Joanna Cole, illustrated by Maxie Chambliss
HarperCollins, 2006

Big Girls Use the Potty!
DK Publishing, 2005

Big Boys Use the Potty!
DK Publishing, 2005

Wash Your Hands!
by Tony Ross
Kane/Miller Book Publishers, 2006

third is your child entering the bathroom. This sequence of photos will continue right up to the final hand washing and drying and leaving the bathroom afterward with a look of pride. Yes, a picture of poo and wee-wee in the potty will make a gleeful addition to your homemade book! And happy Mummy and Daddy faces are a great ending.

Glue these pictures onto pages made of strong paper or poster board, and tape them together in book format using strong packing tape. Narrate the action using simple sentences. Read this book to your child either prior to potty runs or while he is sitting on the potty.

Making the book an interactive adventure will give it even more value. Simply leave empty spaces on each page or place a handful of blank pages at the end. Allow your child to add a sticker or draw a happy face into his book after each successful bathroom visit.

I guarantee that your child will enjoy having his own special book, and very likely it will help him enjoy the process. It will be a great way to help your child remember all the steps involved.

Potty Time Book Reading

Reading to a child while she's on the toilet is a common practice. There are two very good reasons for this.

First, young children don't often sit still in one place for very long unless something is holding their attention. Because most children love to read or be read to, this is a great incentive for them to sit patiently.

Second, in order for a child to wee or poo, his sphincter muscles must relax. When a child doesn't want to sit and he's anxious to get back up, these muscles tighten up and elimination is nearly impossible. Listening to a story causes a child to be attentive to you, and his body relaxes. If his bladder or bowel is full, he'll be able to naturally release and go.

Should you read books about potty training? Maybe. Some children enjoy the stories that relate to what they are doing at the moment. Others find that it puts too much emphasis on the process or that it creates performance anxiety. How do you know which to read? Hold up two books and let your child choose.

Sage, three years old

Tell Stories, Chitchat and Sing

In the same way that reading books encourages a child to sit still and relax, telling your child a story, talking about the day, or singing a song brings the same results. Because your child is likely to be hungry for your one-on-one attention (they all are!), this works like a charm. It's also a great way to take advantage of the time you must spend together in the bathroom. If you're going to be there, you may as well relax and enjoy it!

If you have a younger toddler or baby in the house, set up a toy area in the bathroom for your other child. Rotate the toys so that they are always interesting. If you have a baby who's nursing, bring in a chair and nurse the baby while your toddler is doing his potty business. These ideas make bathroom visits enjoyable for everyone.

Make a Potty Poster

There's a lot to learn when a child is just starting out with potty training. You can help your child remember the details of what to do by making her a potty poster.

As with the custom potty book mentioned earlier, take potty-process photos of your child, or cut pictures from magazines. Glue these pictures in sequence on a large piece of poster board or cardboard. Number the action from start to finish. Hang your creation at your child's eye level in the bathroom, perhaps on the bathroom door.

When you are guiding your child to do a practice run, ask her to help you read the poster and follow the actions herself. Ask her, "OK, now what comes next?" And respond with, "Good for you!" when she knows what to do.

You can make the poster even more special by allowing your child to add a sticker to her poster each time

Christian, three years old

she uses the potty. You can either create a blank space for stickers or just let her put them wherever she wants.

These sticker decorations will make her more connected with the poster and also act as fun rewards for potty visits.

Use a Potty Doll

If your child enjoys playing with dolls, stuffed animals or figurines, you may be able to use this to your advantage.

Children often humanize their toys—making them do all sorts of everyday activities from eating to dressing to sleeping—so a child who enjoys this kind of fantasy play would be likely to follow your lead in having her toy learn how to use the potty right along with her.

Simply select a toy to be a potty partner of the day, or purchase a doll that actually drinks and wets and have your child "teach" the doll how to use the potty. It's a good idea to name this little friend and include her in your other play activities so she, too, can stop what she's doing when it's time to go on the potty.

You might even have two such dolls so that you can direct the action with your own doll. This will allow you to instruct your child through all the steps of using the potty, right up to washing hands afterwards. And because children love to play with their parents and are frequent copycats, this can be a fun and effective process. Not to mention that this will give you some lovely quality time with your little one.

A potty doll by itself usually isn't a magic ticket to complete potty training. But when used with other strategies, it can be a great teaching tool for children who enjoy this kind of play.

Tips for Your Little Boy

In most cases it is best to begin potty lessons with your son sitting down to wee. The primary reason for this is that if you teach him to wee standing up, you will be splitting toilet training into two separate jobs: urination and bowel training. The more often your little boy sits

Do Boys Take Longer than Girls to Toilet Train?

You may have heard that little boys finish toilet training later than girls. There does tend to be a difference, but the amount is insignificant in the big picture. Studies show that on average, girls are one to three months ahead of boys, both with displaying readiness skills and with daytime and night-time independence. However, all children are different, and the age range for starting and finishing training is quite broad. Also, because the whole process can take up to a year from start to finish, the difference will not mean much to your family.

Children's individual personality traits, readiness factors, and age at training and the parent's approach are all more significant factors in the timing of toilet training.

to wee, the more likely you are to catch a poo in the process, particularly because they often occur at the same time.

It also makes sense to wait until he is tall enough to easily master the aim into the bowl. Until then, keep your little boy on the potty, and get him in the habit of holding his penis pointed down towards the bowl to avoid having him sprinkle outside the potty. You might also try having him sit and straddle the toilet seat facing backward. It's easier for him to climb up this way, and it also puts him in the proper position for elimination.

Plus you'll avoid the overspray that can wet his clothing . . . and you . . . and the floor . . . and the wall. . . .

A new option has recently appeared on the market—toddler-sized urinal potties. This looks like a miniature version of a regular urinal but has a bucket just like a potty does. If you use one of these, make sure you either put it on an easy-to-clean floor surface or place a plastic mat around the base until your little one masters his aim. The potential problem with teaching a little boy to stand to wee from the start is that it may interfere with bowel training. Children must sit and relax on the potty in order to have a bowel movement, and because BMs often accompany wee, having boys potty train while seated often makes for more effective and easier training.

Once your little guy has begun to master toilet training and is tall enough to reach the toilet bowl easily, you can switch him to standing up at the regular toilet. If your family has been comfortable with family nudity, and if Daddy or a brother is a willing teacher, have one of them show your toddler how this works. You can also toss into the bowl a square of toilet paper, a specially made potty target, or a few Cheerios for him to use as target practice to help him perfect his aim.

As the mother of two boys with excellent toilet seat manners but who have many young friends who lack them, I beseech you: teach your little boy to lift the seat to wee and then to return it to the lowered position when done. If you teach him to make this a habit from the start, he'll always do it that way. Otherwise, women who use the toilet after your son does will get the shocking surprise of landing with a thump on the cold porcelain rim or of sitting on a splattering of urine drops—neither of which is very pleasant, to say the least.

Be Prepared to Get to a Toilet Quickly

Even before your child asks, make sure that you always know where the toilet is when you are out and about in a shop, a bank, a friend's home or anywhere else. This way, you can move quickly when your little one announces the need to go.

A child who is new to this potty business may wait until the last moment to announce a need to go. When your child says she has to go, get to the potty—and do it quickly! While it's sometimes annoying to have to stop everything to take her to the toilet, this is exactly what you have been hoping to achieve. Your child is recognizing the urge and delaying elimination until she gets to the toilet. So be patient and supportive, even when the urgent quest results in a dry run.

Get a Jump Start to Success

If your toddler is excited about potty training and seems to be getting the hang of it, or if you have a potty deadline you must meet, you can help speed up the process.

Pick a day when you will be home all day and will have no outside pressures. Give your child lots of salty snacks (but do not repeat regularly), and juice or water to drink. Watch him carefully for signs that he needs to go, or set a timer or keep a log so that you remember to do a potty run every thirty minutes or so. Try to think of ways to make this a fun game.

More liquid in means more liquid out, so you'll have plenty of practice visits to the toilet. And we all know that practice makes perfect!

Get Everyone on the Same Track

If your child spends time in someone else's care, make sure that everyone communicates with each other regarding your child's potty training. Have a clear plan for potty training so that everyone is consistent when working with your child. (For information on potty training at nursery or at a childminder's, see page 138.)

Offer a Prize

If you are not certain that your child is physically ready for potty training, I would advise against using any kind of prize system. If he is physically unable to use the potty on his own, you'll just be setting him up for disappointment.

If, however, your toddler is ready physically for potty training but is reluctant emotionally or adapting to the idea slowly, you can help spark the excitement with stickers or "potty prizes". No matter what you've thought about giving children prizes as rewards in the past, there are times to use this effective idea—and potty training is one of those times. According to some polls, more than 80 per cent of parents have given their children rewards or prizes for using the potty, so you'd be in good company.

My surveys have uncovered the fact that most toddlers and preschoolers can be highly motivated to make changes when offered prizes—which, I'm sure, is no great surprise to you! There are several approaches you can use.

The Sticker Plan

Using colourful stickers as rewards is a popular choice among parents and children. Your child can place stickers on a piece of poster board, in a sticker book or on a calendar posted in a visible spot on the wall (preferably near the potty). Another place where your child can put these stickers is right on the potty! This is great fun for a little one and personalizes the seat even more. Invite your child to add a sticker each time he successfully uses the potty. The stickers alone are often enough fun to motivate a child.

If your child requires a bit more incentive, set things up so that a certain number of stickers earns a prize (whatever number you want it to be, but not so many that your child loses interest during the wait; you may want to start off with a small number—say, three stickers—and work your way up, maybe to ten or so). When the magic number of stickers is on the chart, your child gets a prize. This can be a trip out for an ice-cream cone, a small toy or a special privilege.

The Potty Prize Treasure Box

Many parents have reported wonderful success with this colourful idea. Here's how it works:

1. Buy about thirty inexpensive little prizes. (Check the toy shop's party bag aisle for a great selection of inexpensive trinkets. "Pound shops" are good sources for little rewards, too.)
2. Wrap each prize separately in colourful wrapping paper.

3. Put the prizes in a clear plastic bowl on the bathroom counter. Call it the Potty Prize Treasure Box, or some other fun and enticing name.
4. Tell your child, "These are *potty prizes*. You'll get one each time you do your business in the toilet. But no hurry—whenever you're ready."

Most kids are "ready" immediately, but don't be surprised if your child drools over the prize bowl for a few days before deciding to be ready.

Allow your child to choose one prize each time he goes. By the time the prize bowl is empty, the habit will be firmly in place. If your toddler requests a prize after the Treasure Box is empty, ask him to find some of his old prizes and tell him you'll wrap them up again. (Truly. The fun is in the unwrapping!)

After a while your child will begin to forget to ask for a prize, and you can easily move on to the "no-prize" phase.

Make Hand Washing a Fun Part of the Potty Routine

Washing hands after using the toilet is a major deterrent to the spread of germs and infection, yet research shows that many *adults* don't routinely wash their hands after toilet visits, and many don't do an adequate job of washing when they do it. While 95 per cent of men and women surveyed *say* they wash their hands after using a public toilet, about half actually do it, according to the results of an observational study. (Makes you wonder *who* researches these things.) Women surveyed

Asher, two years old

were significantly more likely than men to *say* that they
wash their hands.

"Hand washing is the simplest, most effective thing
people can do to reduce the spread of infectious
diseases," according to Dr Julie Gerberding, director of
the Hospital Infections Program, Centers for Disease
Control and Prevention.

You can instill this healthy lifelong hand-washing habit in your child by making it a standard part of the potty visit each time, whether he makes a deposit or not. Most children love to play and splash in the water, so with a little encouragement, your child will happily adopt this ritual.

Make certain you have a sturdy step stool so that your child can easily reach the sink. Select colourful soaps, foam soap dispensers or child-friendly soaps. You might even have several available so that he has a choice about which to use. Don't rush it. Make sure he lathers up, which can be great fun. Supervise a thorough rinsing, and have an easily accessible towel for drying off.

You can encourage your little one's independence by teaching him how to do this on his own.

Relax About Accidents

Accidents are going to happen during the training period. Use the same approach you use when she buttons her sweater the wrong way or spills some milk. "Oops. Missed the potty that time. Don't worry. Pretty soon, you'll get it right every time."

Accidents are very normal, especially at the start of training. However, if your child is having far more accidents than successes, or if either you or your child is getting distressed about these accidents, you may want to retake the readiness quiz to see if perhaps you've started a bit too early.

Accidents are inevitable at first, but they should gradually decrease. If they continue long after your child has completed training, however, you might want to examine the reasons for them. If your child is simply too busy to stop her activity to get to the bathroom, perhaps you're making it too easy for her to recover from these episodes. You might want to get her more involved in the cleanup process. Teach your child how to help wipe up any mess, change her own clothes, and put her dirty things in the laundry. If she has to help you take care of all of this, it may help reduce these accidents. If busyness isn't the reason, look over the suggestions in Chapters 7 and 8, which cover common potty training problems.

It's typical for a child to master one aspect of potty training before another, so don't be surprised if accidents happen for a while. Just keep praising her successful efforts and keep working on the less-consistent process.

Offer Praise and Encouragement—but How Much?

If you research this seemingly simple question, you'll get adamant advice on both ends of the spectrum. Some experts say that you should give lots and lots of positive feedback, including a partylike atmosphere—even with noisemakers, cake and party hats. Others say that you should avoid getting overly excited or emotional and simply acknowledge that your child's done well.

The right answer is that the *right answer* is different for every parent and child pair. Some parents are naturally more enthusiastic about everything their children do; others tend to be more reserved. Some children

Mother-Speak

"I think you should remind parents on every single page of this book to be calm and patient, since that's the hardest part of toilet training!"

—Patti, mother of twenty-nine-month-old Maddison and four-month-old Mason

thrive on their parents' energy, other children are easily overwhelmed. Even two different children in the same family will respond better to different levels of enthusiasm.

Probably the best advice is to do what comes naturally. What's most important is that you want your child to know that you support him, that you are proud of his efforts as well as his successes.

One More Reminder to Be Patient

This whole process takes time. You probably won't feel confident to completely turn over your child's toileting to him for many months. So relax, be patient and enjoy the journey. Children are only little for a very short time—embrace every moment.

6

Bed-Wetting

When your child uses the toilet all day, every day, with only rare mistakes, you can consider your toilet training job complete, even if your child still wears a nappy to bed. Potty training is about daytime toilet habits. Night-time dryness is a totally separate subject.

> **Doctor-Speak**
> "Toilet training is accomplished when a child uses a potty or toilet for bladder and bowel functions during waking hours."
>
> —**Dr Barton D. Schmitt**, *Contemporary Pediatrics*, **2004**

No Place for Punishment or Shame

I was talking with a friend about this book, and the topic of bed-wetting came up. She told me this story:

"Not too long ago, my friends and their son stayed at our home as houseguests. After dinner the talk turned to parenting issues. The father said that his son, William,* had

---

*Name has been changed.

still been wetting the bed in nursery/pre-school. 'A few spankings, making him sleep in his wet bed, and hanging up his wet sheets in the morning for everyone to see, and we stopped that in short order,' he bragged. That night, around 2 A.M., I woke to hear the kids still chattering away downstairs, as kids having a sleepover often do. The following morning I was up early, at about 5:30, and went down to make coffee. William was sitting on the sofa, reading. 'What are you doing up so early?' I asked. 'I never sleep much,' he said. By the way, did I mention this? William is thirteen.

As clearly demonstrated by my friend's story, the goal to achieve night-time dryness should *never* be part of potty training. The development of night-time urinary control is a biological process. You cannot teach it, and a child cannot control it. Not only is it cruel to punish children for bed-wetting, but such treatment might make the situation worse. It can cause a child to suffer in silence, hiding wet pyjamas and bedding. It can cause psychological trauma or create long-term sleep problems, as in William's case.

As children grow and develop, so does their ability to control their bladder. There is a wide range of "normal" for when a child achieves night-time control. Bed-wetting, called enuresis ("en-yur-EE-sis"), is common among young children, with a higher percentage of boys than girls. Because almost half of all three-year-olds and up to 40 per cent of four-year-olds wet the bed several times a week, it is considered normal behaviour at these ages. Additionally, 20 to 25 per cent of five-year-olds and 10 to 15 per cent of six-year-olds don't stay dry every night.

By the age of nine, only 5 per cent of children wet the bed, and most of those children do it only once a month. As children get older, fewer and fewer have bed-wetting accidents. In the majority of cases, the problem goes away even when parents don't use any special treatment for the condition, and with the small percentage of children who do need help, treatment is relatively simple.

The most common reasons for bed-wetting in a young child are due to his physiology. Your child's kidneys aren't sending a signal to his brain when he's asleep, his brain is too deeply asleep to hear the signals, his bladder hasn't grown large enough to contain a full night's supply of urine, or his system overproduces urine at night. As children grow, all of these conditions self-correct.

Bed-wetting is also hereditary, so if one or both parents were bed wetters, a child has about an 80 per cent chance of doing the same. Diabetes, food sensitivities (specifically to caffeine, dairy products, fruit and chocolate), some medications, or other health conditions can contribute to night-time bladder-control issues. On occasion, bed-wetting can be a symptom of a sleep disorder, so if your child exhibits other signs, such as snoring or restless sleep, you may want to investigate this possibility.

It Is a Natural, Biological Process

No child chooses to wake up cold and wet. Bed-wetting almost never happens because a child is lazy or disobedient. Just like learning to walk or learning to talk, there's a wide range of "normal", and, like other milestones, every child achieves night-time dryness on his own time schedule. There's no reason to rush the process.

For a bed-wetting toddler or preschooler, the solution is simple: allow your child to sleep for naps and night-time in a nappy, padded training pants or disposable absorbent underpants until he begins to stay dry during naps and all night long.

How Do You Know When It's Safe to Go Nappyless?

When your child has been sleeping dry for a week or more, it may be safe to try a night or nap without nappies. Be prepared for occasional accidents at first. A good idea is to double-make the bed. (Use a waterproof pad on top of the bed sheet, and then cover this with a second sheet that can be easily removed if your child wets during the night.) Keep a spare pair of pyjamas close by.

Some children seem to know when a nappy is on their bottoms and use it instead of making a night-time or early-morning visit to the toilet. If your child is daytime independent and you think that she may be ready to go without a nappy during sleep, go ahead and give it a try, if she's willing. As an experiment, have your child go nappyless, sleeping on top of a waterproof pad and double-made bed, to see how she responds. You (and she) might be pleasantly surprised by a dry bottom and a dry bed in the morning.

How to Help Your Child Stay Dry

While it's not necessary to work on night-time dryness when your child is at the toilet training age, you can help a child who *wants* to stay dry at night by doing the following:

- Make sure that your child uses the potty often during the day, about every two hours. This encourages normal bladder function and can help with night-time dryness.
- Direct your child to use the toilet if it's been two hours or if you see signs of the need, such as squirming, wiggling, crotch holding or dancing.
- Avoid providing any food or drinks that act as stimulants, such as chocolate, sugar and caffeine, particularly in the several hours before bedtime.
- Encourage adequate daytime liquids, and limit liquids for an hour or two before bedtime. You don't need to cut out liquids entirely, because this only reduces the amount of night-time urine, it doesn't stop the reasons for bed-wetting.
- Make several trips to the toilet before bedtime— one at the beginning of your bedtime routine and once again at the very end, just before lights out. Make certain that your child finishes emptying his bladder by relaxing on the toilet for three to five minutes. An egg timer can help your child know how long to sit. You can keep him company and talk, read a book, or tell a story. Make this part of your bedtime routine.
- Avoid having your child wear nappies or absorbent pull-ups to bed, and use a special

Hannah, two years old

mattress cover instead. Absorbent pants or nappies can sometimes delay the normal development process because a child can't feel when urination occurs, and it may also give him a subconscious message that it's OK to urinate in bed because he's wearing his pull-ups.

- Use positive reinforcement with a sticker chart to help your child monitor his success.
- Keep a night-light on so the path to the bathroom will be well lit, and give your child permission to use the bathroom during the night if he needs to. Just the subconscious message may help.
- Avoid placing any blame on your child, and don't make him feel guilty or ashamed. Let him know that wetting during sleep is normal and will take time to change.

When Should You Seek Help?

You only need to talk to a doctor about bed-wetting if your child is seven years of age or older or if there are other symptoms of a sleep disorder (such as restless sleep or snoring). However, if your child is younger than seven but bed-wetting is causing either her or you distress, or if you also see daytime toilet problems, you should talk about your concerns with your doctor or another professional.

Many young children who are dry at night for a long period of time begin to wet the bed again. This is sometimes caused by stress or a time of change in their life, or sometimes this is due to a medical reason, such as a bladder or kidney infection. If your child suddenly has a change in her night-time or daytime bladder or bowel habits, it's a good idea to check with your doctor to make sure she doesn't have an infection or another health issue.

With children for whom bed-wetting is a problem, help is a phone call away. A specialist can help you solve the issue with the use of a bed alarm, bladder-training exercises, diet changes, therapy or medication. You can call your doctor, who will refer you to a paediatrician, or you can contact the Enuresis Resource and Information Centre (www.eric.org.uk).

Don't Worry

There are plenty of things we parents must worry about and strive to change, but usually, during the toddler and preschooler years, bed-wetting isn't one of those things. All you have to do is be patient. In time it's very likely your child will be dry at night without your having to be involved in a solution at all. And if your child continues to wet the bed after nursery, know that it is not his fault, and it can be solved respectfully with the help of a professional.

7

Solving Common Toilet Training Problems

Even if you've been thoughtful, patient and organized, toilet training may not go according to plan. There are lots of typical problems that crop up during the training process. The most common problems are training resistance, excessive accidents, refusal to have a bowel movement on the potty, constipation and setbacks. The best place to begin is to contemplate the most usual reasons for toilet training problems and see if you can't figure out the cause of the difficulty. Review the list on the next page to identify your areas of concern (you may have several), and then review Chapters 2 to 4 with your insight. This chapter will provide specific ideas and solutions for the problems that these situations cause during the potty training process.

Solving Any Toilet Training Problem

The first step to solving any problem is to take a deep breath and repeat after me: "My child *will* learn how to use the toilet. They all do. This too shall pass." More than 98 per cent of children master daytime toileting by the age of four, and with patience and the right plan of action, your child will get there, too.

The Most Common Reasons for Toilet Training Problems

- The child is not ready (lacks the appropriate physical skills).
- The child is not ready (emotionally, socially or behaviourally).
- The child doesn't understand what he's supposed to do (communication).
- The child has become too distracted with something else to care about going potty.
- The child is bored with training.
- The child is fearful of, or uncomfortable with, some aspect of training.
- There is a power struggle between the child and the parent.
- There's too much stress and pressure surrounding the process.
- The parent has unrealistic expectations.
- The parent is not following a toilet training plan; it's hit or miss.
- The parent is not ready (lacks time, patience or desire to carry out a plan).
- The parent and caregiver don't agree on a plan and are sending mixed messages.
- The parent is confusing normal accidents with failure.
- The routine doesn't match the child's elimination pattern.
- The approach used doesn't suit the child's learning style or personality.
- The approach used doesn't suit the parent's personality or teaching style.
- There is a physical or medical deterrent (such as constipation, infection or uncontrolled allergies).

Another important concept to understand is that you can lead a child to the potty, but you can't make her fill it. This is your child's undertaking, not yours. You can teach her, you can prepare the necessary tools, and you can be positive and supportive, but—perhaps for the first time in her young life—the ultimate result is 100 per cent in her power.

Keep your perspective. Three of my children are now teenagers, and I'm dealing with driving, dating, the yearn for freedom, high school graduation and college applications. I can tell you that to me, potty training sounds like a big piece of chocolate cake. With a side of ice cream. Sprinkled with chocolates! Perhaps even more surprising is that when I try to remember potty training my toddler, I have a hard time recalling the details—it seems like ancient history. Trust me when I say that a year from now, this will all be ancient history to you, too, and you'll be on to new and interesting parenting adventures.

So, how do we get you from here to there? First, examine the previous list of common reasons for toilet training problems and try to figure out which ones are getting in the way of successful toileting mastery for your child. Once you have a handle on those basic reasons, it will open up your mind to all kinds of new solutions. Then read over any of the topics that follow that match your issues.

Training Resistance

You *thought* your child was ready. You *thought* you were ready. But things are not going according to plan. Following are some common parent statements with explanations and solutions.

"He won't even try!"
If your child seems totally clueless, he probably is. For his entire life he's weed and pooed in his nappy and never even noticed this elimination. Now you want him to not only notice but hold it and then put it somewhere else! It's time to read potty books; make your own potty book (see page 80); have a sibling, friend or parent demonstrate; give a few step-by-step lessons; and maybe even have some bare naked playtime to help him see and feel what's happening down there.

It's possible that your child *has* tried but feels overwhelmed. He may have had high expectations for himself and feels he's failed both you and himself. He may just need help understanding that this isn't a one-day job but will take him a long time to learn. Praise him for the things he can do, no matter how small, and build from those.

I'd also suggest that you retake the readiness quiz in Chapter 2. Ponder each question, and instead of marking down the answer that you hope to be correct, indicate what's really true. Your child may not be ready just yet. And if you already know that, but still need or want to continue training, refill your basket of patience, put a smile on your face, and pull out the fanciest tricks in this book.

"She has tantrums when I make her sit on the potty."
If your child views sitting on the toilet as a punishment, then likely there's been too much stress or pressure for her to learn. If things are really awful, you may need to stop training for a week or two to give both of you a breather. However, if you have made some progress, you may not want to give up what you've achieved. Instead,

make potty time more fun. Add books, toys, music, storytelling or singing to your bathroom visits. Start the fun before she even sits down by having a parade or race into the bathroom. Almost all children thrive with a parent's lighthearted one-on-one playtime, so concentrate on this aspect for a while, without demanding a deposit every time she visits the potty.

When you feel your little one is enjoying potty visits, then begin to take her on a regular schedule of every one and a half to two hours or whenever she looks like she needs to go. When she begins to have success, then praise her and provide her with a sticker or prize. Soon she'll take over and be on her way to independence.

"I've tried everything in the book."

That may be the problem! Your poor little pottier is so confused he doesn't know which end is up! Take a step back and refine your plan. Don't let it get so complicated. Reread Quick Guide 4 to help you clarify your potty training plan so that it is simple and clear.

Excessive Accidents

It's common for children to have accidents when they are new to using the potty. But if accidents don't gradually fade over time, or if your child is having more experience going in her trousers than in her potty, you may think training is going nowhere. Following are a few comments and suggestions.

"He has an accident every day!"

If your child is new to potty training, it is perfectly normal for him to have one or more accidents every single

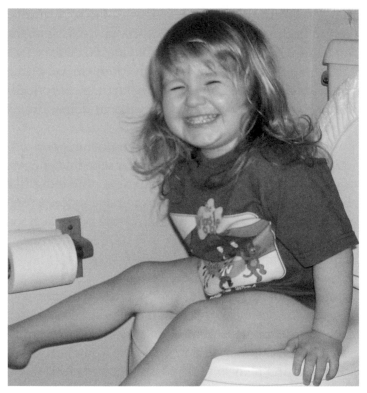

Maddison, two and a half years old

day. Even children who have been trained for six
months or more may have an accident once a week.
The best solution is to be prepared for these with proper
cleaning materials, easy access to a change of clothes,
and a relaxed attitude.

One approach that can help reduce the number of
accidents is for you to become familiar with your child's
signals of impending need (see page 68) and take your
child to the potty when you suspect he needs to go. Do

not *ask* if he has to go, because he is likely to say no. Instead, invite him to follow you, saying, "Let's go and use the potty." Or offer a choice, saying, "Do you want to use your potty or the big toilet?" Or simply take him by the hand and lead him to the bathroom, saying, "Come with me, kiddo."

There's one last thing for you to consider. Do you give your child more attention (good or bad) when he has an accident than when he has success? Turn the tables. Clean up accidents quickly and without emotion, and provide lots of praise, hugs and attention for every productive potty visit.

"She never makes it to the toilet. She usually goes in her pants."

Your child may not be hearing her body when it tells her it's time to go. Or she may get so busy with her play that she tries to wish it away, or she thinks she can hold it much longer than she really can.

You might consider moving the potty closer to her and making it easier for her to go. Create a potty nook near her play area and keep her dressed in very simple clothing. Once she gets used to going when she needs to, you can move the potty back to the bathroom.

You might try having a potty party weekend. Don't announce this to your child—just make a plan in your own mind. Stay home all weekend and hang out in the same room as your little one. Provide lots of salty snacks and plenty to drink. Watch her for signs (see page 68) and get her to the potty as soon as you think she may need to go, plus do a potty run every hour or so. Give stickers, small prizes or treats (how about her favourite crisps?) to keep her motivated and interested. The hidden advantage to this approach is that you can enjoy a weekend of one-on-one quality time with your precious little child.

Constipation and Refusal to Have a Bowel Movement on the Potty

One of the most common and frustrating toilet training roadblocks is when a child willingly wees on the potty but demands a nappy, or uses his pants, for bowel movements. Some children will actually hold their bowel movements and create severe constipation, which further complicates the issue.

Children typically resist having a bowel movement on the toilet, or hold back from going, for one of these reasons:

- Bowel movements take too long to wait for, and an active child dislikes having to sit on the potty for an extended length of time.
- After being used to the squashed sensation of stool coming out into a nappy, the feeling of letting it loose into the air is unsettling and strange.
- A child is used to standing or moving during a bowel movement, and sitting still on the potty is an uncomfortable change of routine.
- Your child thinks the stool is part of him and doesn't understand why he should flush it away.
- A bad experience, such as being splashed on the bottom with urine or water during a movement or having a messy accident, causes a child to avoid having it happen again.

- Pain from a previously difficult or hard stool makes a child afraid to poo on the potty.
- A current case of constipation is preventing usual elimination.

Don't try to solve the problem without understanding why it exists. Once you identify your child's impetus for avoiding bowel movements, you can create the best plan for helping him to have regular and natural elimination. As you put your plan together, consider these basic *don'ts* and *dos*:

What Not to Do

- Don't get angry. Don't scold your child or make her feel ashamed. Your little one isn't doing this on purpose, she isn't trying to make you mad, and she doesn't understand how to solve this any more than you do.
- Don't make your child sit on the toilet and "try" or push. BMs come out when the body is ready, and forcing them can create small tears in the anus (fissures) or haemorrhoids, which cause all-day pain in the rectum. This will cause the child to avoid pooing even more, which leads to constipation, which creates hard stool, which causes more haemorrhoids, and on and on and on to generate a dreadful cycle of pain and frustration.
- Don't let your child strain when he sits to poo. Of course, a little bit of pushing can be necessary for a normal bowel movement. But if he is grunting, straining and forcing, it's a sign that either he's not quite ready to go or he's somewhat constipated.

Have him drink a big glass of water, eat a piece of fruit, and then try again in ten or twenty minutes.

- Don't ever make your child "hold it". When she announces the need to go, or if you notice that her body signals are indicating a need to go, find a toilet immediately. Delaying and holding contributes to constipation and other bowel problems.

What to Do

- Make certain that your child is drinking plenty of fluids all day long. Stick to water and juice (apple, pear, cranberry, grape and prune juice but not orange or other citrus juices).
- Be sure your child eats plenty of fibre-rich foods every day: vegetables (especially raw ones), fruit, whole grains, brown rice and oats are some examples. Avoid giving your child junk food, refined sugar, fizzy drinks, sweets and chocolate.
- Limit foods that can constipate, such as bananas, rice, cheese, citrus juice and carbonated sodas.
- Food allergies or lactose intolerance (intolerance to milk products) can cause constipation in a child. If you suspect this may be true, talk to your doctor.
- If your child has been constipated, apply petroleum jelly or nappy cream to her rectum before potty visits.
- Make sure your child has plenty of daily exercise, which stimulates digestion, prevents constipation, and is necessary for proper elimination.

- Be sure that your child is weeing every one and a half to two hours. Regular urination is a necessary component to regular bowel movements.
- Take your child to the potty first thing in the morning and ten to thirty minutes after a full meal, when BMs are likely to happen.
- Teach your child to go when the urge hits. Explain that the poo is trying to come out and she should go right to the potty.
- Purchase a soft, padded child's adapter seat for the toilet or a potty with a soft seat. Some children find it difficult to sit on the hard surface for the length of time it takes to make a bowel movement.
- If you find your child has had a bowel movement in her trousers, calmly take her to the bathroom. Flush her poo down the toilet with a comment to explain that's where it goes. Have her sit on the potty while you wipe her bottom, and let her know that soon she'll do her poo-poo on the potty.
- If your child will only go in a nappy, begin to have her do so in the bathroom. Progress to having her sit on the potty, in her nappy if she'd like. Once she is used to this, suggest taking her nappy off and putting it into the potty bowl as a "pocket" to catch her poo-poo.
- You might find success by cutting through the crotch of the nappy so that it still is wrapped around her, but the bottom is open to let the poo drop into the potty.
- Make sure that your child sits long enough to empty her bladder or bowel each time she uses the toilet. Make it a relaxing three to five minutes.

Malcolm, twenty months old, and Mummy

- Make sure that your child's legs are comfortable, with knees slightly apart and feet firmly planted on the floor or a sturdy stool.
- Help your child relax on the potty by reading books, telling a story, singing a song, or chatting.
- Have your child close her eyes and take a few deep breaths while you talk or sing softly.
- Play soothing music during potty sits.

- If your child is showing signs of needing to poo but is not having success on the toilet, try having him lean forward and rest his upper body against you while you gently rub his lower back. You can also have him sit backward on the toilet and lean against the tank.
- Read books about using the potty, especially those that talk about poo (yes, really!) such as these:

Whose Poo?
Jannette Rowe
Happy Cat Books, 2005

Poo: A Natural History
Nicola Davies and Neal Layton
Walker Books Ltd, 2005

(This one is aimed at older children but has lots of fun things you can pick out to share with your younger children; it's funny and informative, too.)

Setbacks and Regressing

About 80 per cent of parents report having to deal with toilet training setbacks, which means you are in very good company! There are about a million reasons that children who are having great success with toilet training suddenly go totally backwards. Here are a few of the more common reasons for setbacks:

- There is a change in the family or a disruption in the home, such as moving, a new baby, divorce, marriage, holiday or houseguests.
- The child is bored with the toilet training routine.

- An illness or injury of the child or parent interferes with the usual daily routine for days or weeks.
- There has been a drastic change in routine, such as starting nursery, a sibling going off to school, or an at-home parent going off to work.
- The child has mastered toilet training but then has a number of accidents that erode confidence. Perhaps a particularly embarrassing public episode occurs, or the unthinking comments of a family member or stranger made your child feel inadequate. She may have decided it would be safer if she went back to nappies.
- Your child may have been successful at potty training because you were very successful at reminding him to go at the right times. After a period of success you stopped reminding him, and so accidents began to happen.

Setbacks are always temporary; otherwise, we'd see seven year olds wearing nappies. So when a setback occurs with your child, simply set yourself back, right along with your child, and repeat the actions that were successful for you in the past. For example, if her potty poster was a hit, make a new one. If she was doing perfectly on her potty, but a setback occurred soon after the switch to the big toilet, go back to using the little potty. If she responded to two-hour potty reminders, begin setting a timer to remind her to visit the bathroom.

Tuck away your own injured pride, because this has nothing to do with your job as a teacher nor does it mean your child has failed. It just means your child is normal. Be patient, be supportive, and soon your little one will be back to potty success.

Sapir, two and a half years old

When to Call the Doctor

You should contact your doctor any time you have concerns about your child's health. The following are some of the signs that would warrant a phone call:

- Your child hasn't had a bowel movement in four or more days.
- There is blood in your child's urine or stool.
- Your child has a fever, is nauseous or is vomiting.
- Your child isn't urinating every two or three hours.
- Your child has difficulty starting a stream of urine, even when she has to wee.
- Your child's urine has a foul smell.
- Your child's stomach is extended, hard or swollen.
- Your child's underwear is frequently smeared with stool, and it's unrelated to poor wiping habits.
- Your child is potty trained but suddenly regresses for no apparent reason.
- You are getting excessively angry over the situation. Toilet training problems can be very frustrating and are one of the major causes of child abuse. If you're finding this too much to handle, call a trusted friend or a health care professional.

If your child is having difficulty using the toilet, or if toilet training has become a major issue in your household, your doctor can help you. She may analyze the progress of toilet training, provide you with advice about diet changes, or put your child on a fibre supplement, stool softener or mild laxative, if necessary.

Any child, no matter how healthy, smart or capable, can have toilet training problems. Any parent, no matter how wise or experienced, can need help solving these problems. Don't be shy or embarrassed about seeing a professional about problems with toilet training. This is very common, and professionals talk with parents every single day on this topic.

8

Common Questions and Sensible Answers

Once you enter this new phase in your child's life you'll be faced with unique challenges, many of which you'd never have thought of before you began the potty training process. You'll start to see all things toilet in a new light and realize that even when you feel fully prepared for everything, an interesting new dilemma will appear. Everyday things like flushing noises, public toilets and potty words will require creative problem solving. In this chapter I'll cover the most common situations and provide information and solutions to help you keep your child moving towards toileting independence.

Fear of Flushing

My son is afraid of the flushing of the toilet. How can I help him to get over this fear?

It's not unusual for a child to peer into the toilet and watch the water swirl down the hole to the sound of the loud flush and become confused or fearful about the noise, the hole or the unknown. Children get past this

Matthew, seventeen months old

fear in time, but there are a number of ways to help your child overcome his apprehension.

- For a while, wait until he leaves the room and then flush for him. After a few days or a week, casually flush while in the middle of talking, singing or playing. Don't make it a big deal.
- Chat about what happens when the toilet flushes. Get a book or two from the library about plumb-

ing, or visit a plumbing showroom and do some exploring. (Just watch him carefully so he doesn't use a model toilet!)

- Play a game: stand a foot or so from the toilet, take turns tossing Cheerios into the toilet, and then flush and watch them swirl away.
- Get a copy of the book *It's Potty Time* (Smart Kids Publishing, 2005). It has a potty training story along with a flushing button that generates lifelike sounds along with children's giggles.

Coordinating Two Homes for Training

Our daughter spends half her time at my house and half her time at her father's. How should we approach toilet training to make it less confusing for her?

The more consistent things are in both places, the easier this will be for your little one. If possible, it's great if you could both read the same book or article about toilet training. Decide on an approach and jot down the important points.

Buy two identical potties and keep them in the same place in both homes, such as next to the adult toilet. Purchase duplicate sets of training pants or underwear to be kept at both homes. If you are going to use a chart or potty book, have two of the same, and if you reward with prizes, stickers or treats, do so at both places.

Of course, there are times when two parents do not communicate or agree on issues such as this. In that case be certain that the experience is pleasant and consistent in your home, and be patient. Children are remarkably resilient, and your child will master toilet training even if both situations aren't perfectly aligned.

Travelling with a Newly Trained Child

We finally finished toilet training, and our three-year-old is just now becoming independent. Wouldn't you know it— we have to go out of town for a few days for a family wedding. We'll be driving for six hours and spending a few nights at a relative's home. I'm so afraid our little one will forget everything!

Potty training or no potty training, life must go on! Families are busy. You could never take a whole year off from life, waiting until your child was a master at independent toileting. So first and foremost, take the focus off of the whole potty training issue and enjoy the occasion. Life is far too short not to take joy when it's offered to us, and no matter what, your child will eventually be fully trained and you'll be facing the next adventure in parenting.

Here are a few tips that can help you on your travels:

- Remember that children need to go on the potty every two hours or so. Plan plenty of stops on your drive for using the toilet and stretching those little legs.
- If your child uses a potty, bring it along with you. It can be used in the car, on the side of the road, at an unfamiliar rest stop, and at your relative's home once you arrive.
- Keep several complete changes of clothing with you in the car in case of accidents.

- Cover the car seat with a specially made plastic car seat cover or any protective fabric.
- Maintain as much of your child's normal potty routine as possible: when he goes, where he goes, and how he goes (do you read, sing, talk?).
- Make sure that your child has plenty of fluids and eats a normal amount of fibrous foods (fruit, vegetables, whole grains) to prevent constipation.
- Practise using new toilets before you leave—at a neighbour's or friend's house, a restaurant or a shop—so your child knows that he can use all different kinds of toilets.
- Whenever your child says he has to go on the potty, take him immediately. Politely excuse yourself and your child and whisk him away. Making him wait when he announces the need can either cause an accident or performance anxiety that could stay with him long after your trip.
- Accompany your child on every bathroom visit, because you'll never know what bathrooms are child-safe.

Fathers and Daughters in Public Toilets

When my husband is out shopping or at a restaurant with our daughter and she has to go on the potty, what should he do? She's much too young to go into the toilets alone, and there's no way she can hold it until they get home. I certainly don't want to prevent them from going out together, so what's the solution?

Nielah, fourteen months old

Absolutely, a young child should never go into a public toilets alone, as this is a safety issue on many levels. In addition, you should never entrust your child to a stranger (even if it's an employee of the business) to watch her in the toilet. You are also right not to ask your daughter to hold it, which could lead to an accident or, if repeated, to problems with urination.

It's always been acceptable for mothers to bring both little girls and little boys into public toilets, which tend to be very private with separate toilets for each person. Having Dad bring his daughter into the men's room is a little bit different. To get a solution to this dilemma, I turned to the expert in our house. I asked my husband what he used to do when our two girls were little. He said that it was never a big issue for them. If the men's toilet was a single room, he'd just bring her in with him and lock the door. If the room had an unlocking door and multiple toilets, he'd just scoop her up, tuck her head into his shoulder to cover her eyes, and walk quickly into an individual toilet. He said it was a common sight in men's toilets—dads rushing by with little girls cradled in their arms.

Happily, these days many public places now have "family toilets" intended for nappy changes or for a parent and child to use together. Hopefully these will become more commonplace. You can try to time potty visits to coincide with better toilet options, but this, of course, isn't always possible. Another option for you is to keep a portable potty in the car for on-the-road pit stops.

Public Toilets

Any tips on using public toilets with a potty trainee?
Most young children who are just embarking on the potty adventure love to visit new and different toilets. They like to explore the unique flushers, the unfamiliar

sinks, and the many different paper towel holders and hand dryers. When you can, allow your child a few minutes for this exploration.

Children who are using potties or toilet seat adapters at home may not be comfortable using the big, regular toilets in public toilets. There are folding seat adapters on the market that fit over the seat to give your child a more familiar fit. You can also purchase adhesive seat covers in colourful patterns that are child-friendly and that also protect your little one's bottom from germs.

Keep in mind that if your child is accustomed to using the toilet with his feet on the floor, he may find it difficult to have a bowel movement with his legs dangling in the air. If you're flexible and game, you can kneel on one knee in front of your child and have him put his feet on your leg. Or if the rubbish bin is movable, cover it with a paper towel and let your child use it for a footstool.

Be wary of automatic flushing toilets. These have startled more than one child who has been sitting on the toilet during an unexpected flush. Automatic toilets have an electronic device that registers when a toilet has been vacated. Most children are too short for the device to register properly, and movement can cause the flush. You can purchase a Flush-Stopper, which blocks the toilet's electronic "eye", or hold your hand or a paper towel over the button while your child is on the toilet.

Very often newly trained children wait until the last minute to announce the need to go, and in a public place that could put you at the end of a queue with your child dancing with urgency. Never be afraid to politely ask if you can move to the front of the queue when you are taking a child in need. A smile and a mention that she's newly potty trained will have most people happily allowing you to go first.

Using Portable Toilets with Your Child

Our older son plays baseball, so we spend a lot of time in the spring at various baseball fields. We're just going into ball season, and we're thinking of potty training our younger son but wondering how he'll respond to going in those outdoor porta-potties.

Our three older children play baseball, so we faced this dilemma with our fourth child, Coleton. Because we were quite familiar with the unsanitary and somewhat frightening look of these portable toilets, we made some of our potty training decisions based on the schedule for the season. There are various ways to approach this situation.

If your child is only somewhat ready to begin training, you might want to put off training for a few months, until the sports season is over. That's a simple way to avoid dealing with the issue altogether. Use the next few months to follow the ideas in Chapter 3 to prepare your child to begin active training after the baseball season.

However, if your child is ready for potty training—and you are, too—there are ways to proceed and handle the lack of indoor plumbing.

One must-have product is a folding, portable toilet seat adapter. Buy the biggest one you can find, because many portable toilets have super-sized gaping-hole openings and you want to be certain that the seat is adequately covered. Be sure to place the adapter securely on the seat and also hold on to your child as he uses the toilet. You don't want your child to fall in—that could set back toilet training for ever!

You can bring your child's potty along in the car and place it on the floor in the porta-potty stall, or avoid these delightful little rooms entirely and let your child use his potty in the car.

Another option is to scout out the immediate neighbourhood and find out if a nearby fast-food restaurant or shop has a public toilet you can use when necessary. (Understand that this won't *always* work with a new trainee, who often doesn't announce the need to go until it's urgent.)

Keep in mind that you want to continue to teach your child good hygiene, and many portable toilets don't provide any method for hand washing. Carry a small bottle of hand sanitizer or some wet wipes in your bag to do the job.

Potty Training Twins, Triplets, or Two Children Close in Age

I have twins who just had their second birthday. What do I need to know about potty training the two of them?
Parents who have twins, triplets, or two children close in age sometimes believe that they should train their children at the same time. While this may seem like a time-saver, it doesn't always work out that way, as your children may approach readiness at different times. It's

Father-Speak

"We've made it a rule not to use one daughter's success to inspire the other's, even though it is very tempting to say, 'Your sister is doing it; you can, too.' Competition is already a natural part of their relationship, and this kind of thing can backfire and actually halt progress for the less enthused twin."

—**Jim, father of two-year-old twins Anna and Amy**

always easier to work with a child who is ready and able to tackle the new skill.

I'd suggest that you take the readiness quiz in Chapter 2 separately for each of your children. Don't compare your children to each other or to any other children. When they start training and when they finish it has nothing whatsoever to do with their brilliance or abilities—it simply has to do with their toileting readiness. When the time comes for them to learn to tie their shoes, ride a bike, or do joined up writing, they will be likely to master these skills—as they will many others—at different times. Avoid comparing their skills or commenting in public about the advanced skills of one child over another.

It's likely that if one child is ready sooner than the other, that child will become ready more quickly just by watching and learning from her sibling. So keep your eyes open to watch for signs that readiness is taking a leap forward.

Purchase at least two potties, because you'll want an accessible potty for each child whenever the urge strikes. Also, it's likely that when one is sitting on the potty, the other will think it's a great idea. In addition, once you get in the routine of using the potty after meals, before bed and in the morning, they won't have to wait and take turns, which could invite arguments or accidents.

It can be helpful to set up a play area in the bathroom, with toys or games, so that if one child is using the potty, the other can be patient and happy while waiting for the other. (This is a good tip to keep any younger children happy, too.)

Keep in mind that every child learns differently. Just because a certain method works perfectly for one child doesn't mean it will work for another. Your children may require slightly different approaches as you go through the potty training process, so be open, attentive and, of course, patient.

Potty Training Children with Special Needs

Our daughter has developmental and physical disabilities. Do you have any specific ideas for toilet training a child with special needs?

The things that are most important with potty training apply to every child, no matter their developmental stage or physical skills. Most of the tips and ideas in this book will apply to special needs children exactly as they apply to all other children, because this method is based on understanding your individual child and working with her to master toilet training at her own pace.

In order for training to be a positive experience, it's helpful for your child to have as many of the readiness skills as possible. Children with special needs may not necessarily have *all* the readiness skills though. A child may not be physically able to take her trousers off and on, for example, but still may be ready to begin potty training with a parent's help with this step. Your knowledge of your child's abilities and strengths will override any score on the readiness quiz—or anyone else's opinion, for that matter. In addition, you may be willing to invest the extra time and energy necessary to help your child achieve this confidence and self-esteem building skill.

Shop around for the proper potty or toilet adapter for your child. A soft, padded seat, armrests, side rails, a back support or a special footstool might be helpful. You'll want your child to be comfortable while seated on the toilet.

Children with limited physical abilities might benefit from a bidet (a water spray attachment used for cleaning up after a bowel movement). Portable bidet systems that can be attached to your regular toilet are available. If wiping with toilet paper is exceptionally difficult or impossible for your child, you might want to get a special portable air dryer made for this purpose.

It helps to know your child's pattern of elimination before you begin. If you can note how often your child wees and at what time of the day she normally has a bowel movement, it can help you put together a routine that matches your child's usual schedule.

At the very start, just having your child sit on the potty is success. Set up the bathroom to be a fun and inviting place. Have some pleasant, soothing music playing, and collect an assortment of your child's favourite toys or books to keep in the bathroom. In more complex situations, you might consider using a small television or computer for watching movies.

If your child is sensitive to odours, make sure you have an air freshener or fan to keep the air clean. If your child is touch-sensitive, you may want to use extrasoft toilet paper or flushable wet wipes.

Set the mood so that going to the toilet is a relaxing and pleasant event. The first few potty sits should only be three to five minutes long. If your child tires of the game before that, don't pressure her to stay seated. Remember that you are setting the stage for future visits.

Set up a routine to take your child to the toilet throughout the day. Good times are immediately upon waking, after meals, before bath, before leaving the house and before bed. Once your child is familiar with this routine, add a few additional potty sits throughout the day. Give your child specific step-by-step instructions. You may want to create a detailed potty poster, as described on page 84.

Watch your child carefully for signs that she has to go to the toilet. When you notice that your child is giving signs, do your best to get her there promptly. If it takes longer to get your child on the potty because of a wheelchair or other equipment, try to keep an eye on her so that you can get her to the potty before the need is so great she has an accident.

If you use a potty, keep a piece of toilet paper in the potty so you know if even a few drops make it into the bowl. If you are using a seat adapter on a regular toilet,

> ### Mother-Speak
> "Our daughter responds very well to music, so we made up a potty song. 'This is the way we wee and poo, wee and poo, wee and poo. This is the way we wee and poo, on the little potty!' The second verse is, 'This is the way we wipe our tush . . .' The final verse happens during hand washing: 'This is the way we wash our hands . . .' We sing the song every time we have her sit on the potty, and it keeps her seated long enough to have success, and then it helps her remember all the other steps in the process."
>
> **—Karen, mother of three-year-old Lisa**

listen carefully and watch your child's expressions to see if you can tell when she's urinating. Any small success can be rewarded with praise, hugs and a small treat or prize.

If your child is taking any regular medications, talk to your doctor about possible side effects that might affect elimination and how you might offset this. Some medications, for example, tend to cause constipation, which can often be handled with proper diet.

Take potty training one small step at a time. When your child feels comfortable at one level of skill, then move on to the next one. Be patient and supportive all along the way, and be confident that every day brings you closer to success, even those days when it doesn't feel like it! You may occasionally take one step forward and two steps back, but eventually your child will master toilet training.

Talk to your doctor or with parents of children who have similar needs as your child and see if they have any particular ideas to share. There's nothing like talking with someone who's been there before you.

Nursery and Potty Training

Our son goes to nursery three days a week. How can we ensure a good toilet training experience?

Most nurseries are well organized for helping parents with toilet training, and they have lots of experience. Before you begin toilet training, talk with your provider and ask how they normally handle it. Discuss the factors that are most important to you, and ask any questions you have.

You will need to understand that handling toilet training with more than one child in a group setting is very different than doing it one-on-one at home. Providers may have specific routines that work well for them. If you disagree with any part of the plan, it's best to be polite and respectful as you explain why you would like your child's training to be handled differently and to offer to do what you can to make it easier for your provider.

Having a partnership between you and your nursery provider will make the experience more pleasant for everyone involved. Keep the lines of communication open, and when you have questions or concerns, address them immediately. Keep in mind that any problems should be discussed privately, not in front of a child, who may misunderstand or become concerned about what she hears.

Once you know how the nursery or childminder approaches potty training, try to set up a similar situation at home. The more consistent you are in both locations, the more likely your child will go along with the plan.

Bad Language and Potty Humour

How do you deal with inappropriate toilet-related jokes? For example, lately my son is obsessed with bodily waste. The other day when he was having a BM on the potty, he said to my husband, "My poo is like toothpaste squeezing out, but it's brown." Then he started laughing and asking over and over if we wanted him to put it on our toothbrushes. Now he keeps calling his brother poo-poo-paste, because he thinks it's very funny. Obviously we don't!

Potty training invites all sorts of strange comments from our children, things that we may consider improper or rude. It also introduces children to words that accurately describe waste but when used out of the bathroom become "bad" words. Like it or not, though, kids can be unashamedly honest, and they tell it like it is! Further, children find private body parts, waste products and body sounds hysterically funny.

Many children (and some adults and stand-up comedians) go through the phase of using toilet topics as humour. While normal, it can be quite annoying, not to mention embarrassing when used in public, so the sooner you take action, the sooner it will stop.

Without adding anger or shaming to the situation, teach your child what is socially appropriate. When your child makes a joke or rude comment, stay calm, look him in the eye, and say in a serious voice, "That's not polite to say." Or, "That's not something we joke about in this house." Or, "Bathroom words need to stay in the bathroom."

Keep in mind that your child will probably still use toilet humour with his friends, because they are all at similar developmental stages. Also, don't forget that young kids are great mynah birds. If parents, friends and movies demonstrate toilet talk as humour, kids will do the same. While you can't eliminate all this from your child's life, you can discuss what they hear and let them know that even if others use toilet talk, it's still not polite to do so in public.

Refining Your Little Boy's Aim

How do I get my five-year-old son to aim better? He misses the toilet half of the time and wees on the floor!

There are a number of reasons that little boys miss the toilet. Often it takes too long to wee and they get bored, so they begin to look around—and the body follows their eyes and head, so they miss the toilet.

On occasion, a toddler is too small to be standing up to urinate, which makes it difficult for him to aim properly. If this is the case with your son, you can have him sit backwards on the seat to wee until he's a little taller.

Your son might be waiting too long to use the toilet, and then he has to rush to get to the bathroom, so he's hurrying to get his trousers down. To complicate matters, once he starts going, the force of his stream is strong, causing a wild spray and splashes.

Sometimes the problem is simply that no one has shown him how to point his penis down to keep the

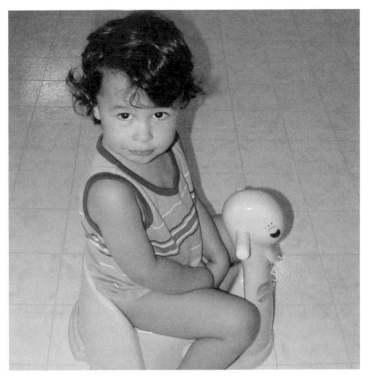

Kahlil, two years old

spray directed properly into the bowl. A discussion and demonstration, followed by several reminders, can solve this.

Whatever the case, it's annoying to have to constantly clean little puddles off the floor! Further, letting this continue without addressing it may create bad habits.

First, I would suggest that you talk to your son about the importance of aiming into the toilet, and point out what happens when he doesn't. You might even use some fun aiming ideas, such as throwing a few Cheerios or potty-time targets into the bowl.

Finally, get him involved in the cleanup. Have him help wipe up his own mistakes, and he'll quickly learn to aim into the bowl.

As long as we're on this topic, here's a reminder to teach your little guy from the start to lift the lid all the way up before weeing and then lower it back down when he's done. It prevents unpleasant surprises for the next person using the toilet and, if taught from the start, will become a very polite habit.

Urinary Tract Infections (UTI)

My little girl has been using the toilet more often than usual the past few days, but each time she goes just a little bit or sometimes not at all. She's also complaining that it hurts when she wees. Could she have an infection?

It is very possible this is the case. Infections of the bladder and kidney are common in young children, particularly girls. These infections are caused by bacteria and are usually not contagious.

Whenever you suspect an infection, you should make a call to your doctor, who can help you determine if there is an infection. Some of the most common signs of a urinary tract infection are:

- frequent, small-volume urination
- an urgent need to urinate resulting in a dry run
- painful urination, often described as "burning"
- blood in the urine
- a fever

- abdominal pain or tenderness
- lower back pain
- urine that has an unusual or foul odour
- fussiness and irritability

A medical professional will review your child's symptoms, examine your child, and take a urine sample to determine if an infection is present. If it is, antibiotics will likely clear things up quickly.

While you can't totally prevent your child from ever getting a urinary tract infection, the following may reduce the likelihood:

- Make certain you teach your daughter to wipe from front to back to avoid spreading bacteria.
- Keep your uncircumcised boy's foreskin clean.
- Change nappies, training pants or underwear as soon as they are wet or soiled.
- Make sure your child urinates often, and avoid having her hold it if she has to wee.
- Encourage your child to sit on the toilet long enough to empty her bladder.
- Avoid giving your child soapy bubble baths.

Handling Unwanted Advice

My grandmother is on a campaign for us to potty train our daughter. She claims that in her day, all children were potty trained by their first birthday, and our daughter is almost two! Here's the problem: we don't think our daughter is ready, and we know we aren't either. How do we handle the friction over this issue?

This is definitely one of those issues that are a reflection of the times. Fifty years ago more than 90 per cent of children were potty trained by eighteen months of age. To be clear, I should actually rephrase that to make it more accurate: 90 per cent of *mothers* were reliably putting their children on the toilet by the time their children were eighteen months old. In today's world, unless a family is practising infant elimination communication, the average age for a child to *begin* potty training is a wide span from eighteen to thirty-two months of age, with completion occurring between the ages of two and a half and four. Today the most common indicator of when to begin potty training is a child's readiness to begin. However, this evolution of approaches may be something the other generation doesn't know about or doesn't agree with.

You can respond to unwanted advice from your grandmother, or from anyone else who has a different viewpoint on potty training, in a variety of ways. The method that you choose will depend upon your personality, your mood, and your relationship with the advice giver. Here are a few options:

• **Provide information.** You may want to acknowledge to her that things were done differently when she was raising her children. Explain that today's research tells us that potty training is easier and less stressful for everyone if you wait until a child is physically and emotionally capable of actively participating in the learning process.

• **Quote a doctor or a book.** Many people accept your point of view if a medical professional or published book has validated it. Simply say, "My doctor said to wait a few more months before we start training." Or, "I'm currently reading a book on the topic to set the best plan for us."

- **Tell her that you're starting.** Lots and lots of pre-potty training activities are outlined in Chapter 3, and it's likely you're already doing some of these. Mention that you've already started the process.

- **Politely disregard.** This is a helpful approach if you know that there is no convincing the other person to change her mind—she has already raised her children this way and is imparting "you should, too" kind of advice. Simply smile, nod and make a noncommittal response, such as, "Really? Interesting!" Then go about your own business in your own way.

- **Steer clear of the topic.** If you've tried to educate or disregard to no avail, then diversion or distraction is definitely in order. Whenever the topic comes up, swiftly change the subject: "Would you like a cake? I just bought them and they're delicious. . . ."

Playing with Poo

I'm embarrassed to even ask this question, but I will. I walked in on my newly potty trained son, and he was finger painting with his poo! He had taken it out of the potty and spread it all over the floor. I was really shocked, and I yelled at him the whole time I cleaned it up. I'm still worried about it. Is this normal behaviour?

Yes, believe it or not, this is perfectly normal behaviour. Children don't have the same inhibitions and distaste

Orrin, nineteen months old

that we adults have about normal bodily waste. A newly potty trained youngster may be intrigued with what his body has produced and be curious about it. Many wave bye-bye to their stool before they flush, and it's not unusual for a child to call a parent to show off a particularly interesting creation in the toilet! Some even go so far as to touch or taste their final product, something we adults find distasteful. (Bad pun intended.)

The best way to handle this is to keep your own emotions in check and explain to your child what we do and don't do with our waste. Tell him that poo has germs in it that don't belong on hands, and then wash him up thoroughly. Supervise your child when he uses the toilet for a while to be sure he doesn't give in to the urge to finger paint again.

Constipation

My son gets constipated, mainly because his diet is very limited. He only eats pasta and cheese, peanut butter and jam sandwiches, and biscuits or cakes! He won't go near fruit, vegetables or whole grains. Any ideas?

In this case it is right to assume that diet is the reason for his constipation. This can delay potty training, and it can cause health problems as well. It is important to work healthier foods into your child's diet. Until he grows out of this picky-eating stage, you can do this in creative ways to get past his choosy palate. Here are a few ideas:

- Substitute half of his regular pasta with whole wheat pasta. When mixed with the cheese sauce, he likely won't even notice it.
- Make his sandwich with one side of his regular bread and one side with whole wheat bread. Place it on his plate with the familiar bread facing up. Substitute high-sugar jam with all-fruit spread. Add a side dish of fruit or veggies.
- Make homemade ice-lollies out of fruit and vegetable juices, pureed fruit and vegetables (apple and carrot is a good mix), or yogurt. Kids love ice-lollies, and your son will think he's getting a treat, when you'll know it's good for him.
- Shop around for healthier biscuits or cakes—you can find some made with carrots, bananas or courgettes. Or make these at home so that you can control the ingredients.
- Present fruit or vegetables cut into bite-sized pieces with a sauce for dipping, such as yogurt or salad dressing.

Training an Active Toddler

My active daughter won't sit still for a moment! Getting her to stay put on the potty long enough for something to happen is a real challenge. How do I get her to stay seated?

For some active children, when potty training first begins, it's all about keeping them seated long enough to catch a bit of success. After a few successful episodes, your child will understand the purpose for sitting on the potty, and she'll likely be more cooperative.

For your child to have success on the potty, she must sit still and her body must be relaxed. You can help her by doing any of the following while she's seated:

- Read to her.
- Sing with her.
- Tell stories.
- Give a puppet show.
- Paint her fingernails or toenails.
- Play word games, such as I spy.
- Listen to music or a child's audiobook.
- Chat about the day.
- Set an egg timer to indicate how long she should sit.

You can also encourage success by offering your child lots of fluids and then taking her to the potty when she's most likely to go—when she first wakes up, every one and a half to two hours throughout the day, twenty to forty-five minutes after drinking, plus anytime she gives signals that she needs to go (see page 68).

Don't force a new trainee to sit so long that she becomes upset or angry. This will just backfire and make the whole potty training process miserable for everyone.

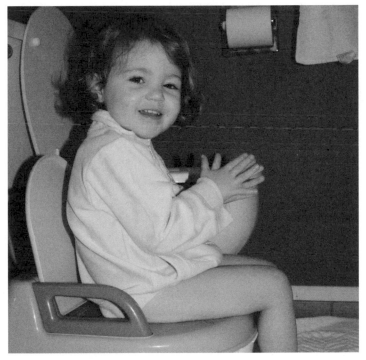

Arianna, two years old

Instead, be patient, make the experience joyful, and you
will eventually have potty success.

Celebrations and Rewards

*Every time my son has a successful deposit in his potty, we
have a little victory dance and he gets a small prize. He's
making great progress, and we're having fun, too, but my
friend told me that she never made such a big deal over it
with her kids and they are both trained. Should I stop the
celebrations?*

Children are different from one another, just as adults are different from each other. Some children respond beautifully to celebrations and prizes, and it makes training a pleasant, rapid and successful endeavour. On the other hand, some children feel pressure to perform or feel that every small act deserves a big prize, thus causing the effort to not go as planned. And while some parents enjoy the party atmosphere, other parents don't want to approach training in this way.

There is no one right answer to the question of whether to use prizes and celebration or to approach training with a matter of fact acceptance. Success comes differently for each child. Just as in many aspects of parenting, you know your child best and you should proceed in the ways that work best for you and your family. So if you and your son are enjoying your little potty parties, then go right ahead and celebrate!

Fascination with New Toilets

My son has recently mastered potty training. We're having a real problem with him constantly asking to use the toilet. Any restaurant, shop or friend's home that we visit requires repeated visits—with little actual use! He also interrupts our conversations to ask to be taken to the toilet. What should we do?

The first thing you should do is congratulate yourself and your son for doing such a great job with potty training! Your little one understands that no matter what he's doing, he should stop when he has the need and find a toilet. Because this is all so new to him, he may not yet be reading his body signals clearly, meaning he'll often have a dry run or two.

He's also just learning that no matter where he is, there is a toilet close by. He's discovered that every toilet looks and functions differently. This can be a bit confusing. In addition, being curious and interested as children are, the novelty of visiting new toilets is a grand adventure.

Most often the best approach here is to simply be patient. You really *do* want your child to continue to let you know when he has to use the toilet, and you want him to go anytime he feels he should. The novelty of this newly discovered power usually passes quickly, and your child will learn to recognize and respond to his body signals. Relax. All this practice will pay off. Soon your child will only be requesting a toilet visit when one is truly needed.

Stalling Bedtime with Potty Visits

Since we've started potty training, it's become the number one stall tactic for avoiding bedtime. It seems like every night after my son has been tucked into bed, he has to get up once or twice to use the toilet.

It may be a stall tactic, but it also may be his biology. Your child likely gets through the bedtime routine, including a visit to the potty, but then asks to get back out of bed to use the toilet five or ten minutes later. It's possible that he may not feel the need to urinate when he's walking around, but the minute he lies quietly in bed his bladder relaxes and calls out to him. So he really *didn't* have to go before, but he really *does* need to go now.

And yes, your son *may* have discovered that the one way he can—for sure—get you to stop the bedtime process is to announce that he has to go on the potty. The solution is to take him when he asks but make it brisk and businesslike. Avoid chitchat or any pit stops for something to drink or for picking up a toy. Just get him right back to bed. This way extra toilet trips will lose their appeal.

Frequent Potty Visits

We're really proud that our daughter is doing such a great job with potty training. However, she seems to have to make use of the toilet every hour or so. Then when she goes, she often doesn't wait until she's finished. She jumps up too soon, so she ends up weeing on her pants!

A common reason for frequent potty visits is that your child isn't relaxing on the toilet long enough to empty her bladder completely. Children are much more interested in going off to play than sitting on the toilet, so pit stops and incomplete voiding are common occurrences. The problem, of course, is that your child will just finish going but quickly have the urge to go again, or, as in this case, she'll stand up before she's even finished weeing!

In addition, some children drink fluids in small amounts throughout the entire day, which is very healthy but, of course, leads to more frequent potty visits.

Furthermore, busy parents often rush children, telling them, "Hurry up! It's time to leave!" This causes their

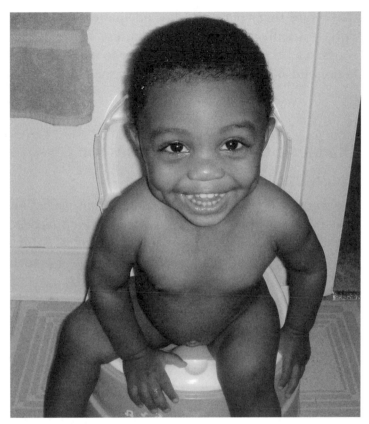

Avery, twenty months old

children to get into the habit of rushing toilet time, which results in incomplete voiding.

If these frequent potty visits are something new in your house, your child might have a urinary tract infection. Check out the list of symptoms earlier in this chapter.

If your child is healthy but active, the solution to these pit stops, dribbling and frequent toilet trips is to make sure that your child has adequate time on the potty—usually two to three minutes. You can sing songs, read books, or use an egg timer to make sure that your child sits long enough to void completely.

Bladder-Stretching Exercises for Accident Control

My daughter is working on potty training, but she has lots of accidents. My aunt said we should work on bladder-stretching exercises: having her hold it as long as possible before having her use the toilet. Is this a good plan to strengthen her bladder muscles?

Having your child delay urination when she has the urge to go very likely won't solve the accident problem and could easily create more problems for her. According to the American Urological Association (urology health.org):

> Children who hold their urine deliberately during the daytime may not help their situation at all. Rather than "stretching out the bladder," using these techniques in children promotes delaying of normal urination and may lead to subsequent urgency and daytime wetting.

There are a number of techniques that really do help your child avoid daily accidents. Here are a few ideas:

- Have her use the toilet on a regular basis, every one and a half to two hours or twenty to forty-five minutes after drinking.

- Tell, don't ask! Avoid asking a busy child, "Do you have to go on the potty?" (And stop my playtime? No, thank you!) Just take her by the hand and say, "Let's go to the potty."
- Give less attention for accidents (clean them up matter-of-factly), and give more positive attention for successes.
- Help your child relax while she is sitting on the toilet by reading to her, telling a story, chatting or singing. (Tight, anxious muscles won't release urine.)

Handling His Penis While on the Potty

Frequently when I put my son on the potty, he reaches right down and plays with his penis. I am not sure what to do about it!

First, make sure that your son's private areas are always kept clean. Check to be sure that he doesn't have a dirt buildup in the creases or an infection. Undress him for his bath and examine him for any redness, rash or crustiness. If you spot anything, give your doctor a call and ask about the best solution. The answer may be similar to treatment for nappy rash, such as daily cleaning, changing his pants immediately after wetness or soiling, and applying a healing cream.

Very likely, though, your son is healthy and fine. Often a child whose privates have been continually covered by a nappy or training pants will be happily surprised to find something new down there, something that he wasn't really aware of! He may discover that it feels pleasant when he touches himself or that his new little "toy" responds to touch by changing shape and texture.

Usually this fascination is short-lived. Most often it's simply a matter of distracting your child or giving him a toy to hold and keeping him focused on the reason he's on the toilet.

Embarrassing Bathroom Questions

I'd heard that you should let your child watch you use the toilet, so I let my daughter come into the bathroom with me. I was unprepared, though, when she started asking about my pubic hair and why I have it and she doesn't!

It is common advice to have a child watch you to help teach toilet training. However, most people don't tell you that it's not really necessary for your child to observe every detail. Just seeing you sit on the toilet, even if all your private areas are covered, is enough to give a child the lesson she needs.

If your child *does* see more than you intended and asks questions about what she sees, keep your answers simple and brief. You might say, "Grown-ups have hair, but children don't." Typically, this will be enough to satisfy your curious child, who's likely simply making an observation about what she sees.

Wiping Lessons

How do you teach a child to wipe decently after number two? We have less than a year until pre-school starts, and our daughter can't seem to do a good job. Are we expecting too much?

Learning how to wipe properly is a big job that can be hard for young children to master. Their little arms just don't reach easily, and it takes time and patience to learn, so they often get more on their hands or pants than on the toilet paper. Most children will need help with wiping until the age of four or five.

The best path to wiping independence is to allow your child to take over, a little at a time, in steps.

1. You wipe for her, while talking about what's happening, to teach the process.
2. You wipe first, and then she finishes wiping, with some coaching from you.
3. She wipes first, and then you finish.
4. Finally, she takes over the job on her own.

Show your child how much toilet paper to use, either by counting squares or extending a piece to the floor or out to an arm's length. Explain that it takes two or three wipings after a poo to clean it all off and that she should wipe until there is no more brown colour on the paper. (If you have a septic system, teach her to flush after the first wiping, to prevent clogging problems.)

A great product for helping young children to wipe better is flushable wet wipes. These are softer than toilet paper, and the wetness makes for a cleaner bottom. An alternative is for you to dampen a small amount of toilet paper for your child. Finish with dry paper.

Remember to teach girls to wipe from front to back to prevent the transfer of bacteria. And teach boys to give their penis a slight shake after urination so their underpants don't get covered with urine drops.

Faecal Soiling (Encopresis)

Even though we've given our son a number of wiping lessons, we still continually see brown smears on his underwear. He doesn't even seem bothered by this! What could be the problem?

If you believe that your child is wiping well, but you're seeing frequent brown smears on his pants, you may be dealing with something entirely different, called faecal soiling, which is often brought about by constipation. It's not uncommon for children to ignore the stains and even the odour—they can become used to these and fail to even notice them.

Constipation is a common cause of faecal soiling. Children who are not having regular bowel movements can become constipated. Children who are constipated have hard stools that are painful to pass. These problems can lead to a buildup of pressure, resulting in some leakage into their pants. If this continues without intervention, a child can begin to lose nerve sensation in the area, preventing him from feeling the sensation necessary to identify the need to use the toilet.

Faecal soiling is the *result of a problem*, not the original problem. If you suspect that this is the case with your child, it is important for you to deal with any potty training resistance (see Chapter 7, page 107) or constipation (see Chapter 7, page 112) in order to end the soiling.

If you've ruled out poor wiping skills, potty training resistance or constipation as reasons for soiling, then talk to your doctor. There are other reasons that this can occur, and a professional can help you determine what these are for your child.

Motivating a Child with No Interest in Potty Training

Our daughter is three and a half years old. We introduced the potty concept to her almost a year ago when we bought a Sesame Street potty, a drink-and-wet doll, and prizes. From the beginning, she has loved the idea of putting her dolly on the potty and then "pretending" to go herself. She even wipes, flushes and washes her hands. But not much really happens! We encourage her with gentle, positive words, but we're not making any real progress. She thinks it is a game. She's physically ready and able, but, sadly, she is losing interest in wanting to sit down all that often. Should we just put it all away and wait until she's ready?

When potty training is introduced, many children view it as a game—particularly when bright coloured potties, dolls, prizes and playing with water are all part of the event. But how many games will a toddler stay interested in playing many times a day, every day for a year or so? None that I can think of!

In order to help your daughter take potty training seriously, it may be time for you to adjust your view and your approach. Think of it this way: if your daughter lost interest in brushing her teeth, would you just put away her toothbrush until she was ready to use it again? Of course you wouldn't—you would brush those little teeth anyway.

Yes, potty training should be relaxed and pleasant, but just like brushing teeth, there is a point when— happily or not—it just needs to happen.

First, look over the list on page 106 (Chapter 7) to see if you can identify any concrete reasons your child is resisting potty training: is there any trauma, fear,

Arianna, two years old

confusion or other issue blocking her? If you can't come up with anything, then perhaps a change in your attitude will move her along to toileting independence.

Undetected constipation can make elimination uncomfortable and will stand in the way of toilet training success. Make sure that your child's diet supports easy elimination. Limit sugar, sweets and junk food, and provide plenty of fruit, vegetables, beans and whole grains.

Because most young children love to be "big", you may be able to use this concept to motivate her. Capitalize on all the benefits of being a big girl, including freedom from nappies and wearing fancy big-kid pants.

On the other hand, some children relish being your "baby" and fear that if they give up nappies, they must give up other things that they perceive as babyish. If this is the case, let your child know that she can still sit on your lap, be carried, use her dummy or breastfeed at bedtime, and snuggle with you. Reassure her that saying good-bye to nappies doesn't mean she has to be all grown up.

Remember to stay positive, and try to be patient. Your child needs this from you. Eventually she will use the toilet just like everyone else, and this time in your life will just be a blip in your parenting memory book. So take a big breath and remind yourself that this, too, shall pass.

This is just one small aspect of growing up. There are likely lots of wonderful things happening in your child's life right now. Try not to let potty training problems colour your entire existence. Remember to celebrate all the good things that are happening in your family. Be thankful, and count your blessings.

9

Bathroom Safety

After years of changing nappies and months of active participation in your child's potty training process, you are probably looking forward to the day that your child takes over his toileting and becomes independent. It will indeed be a happy day the first time your child stops play—on his own!—and goes to the toilet without involving you at all. Such a step in independence does signal a major step in your child's maturity and is well worth celebrating. However, caution should accompany your celebration. The bathroom can be a very dangerous place for a young child, and even though he's old enough to handle his own toileting needs, he is years away from having the ability to make his own safety decisions. Furthermore, if your new trainee has younger siblings, they will be exposed to the many hazards that await them when the bathroom door is left open. Most childhood poisoning incidents occur with children between the ages of one and five; three-quarters of these poisonings occur in the home.

Once your child begins toilet training, even before he graduates to going alone, you should make sure you've made your bathrooms child-safe. Safety concerns often get missed during the busy potty training process, and they are strangely missing from almost all books on

Sage, three years old

potty training. But it is time—right now, before another day passes—to do your bathroom safety check.

Keep in mind that safety precautions are updated constantly, and because all children, and all homes, are very different, no checklist is fully complete and appropriate for every situation. However, I've worked to make this list as inclusive as possible, and it can help you along as you make all the bathrooms in your home child-safe and ready to welcome your newly independent trainee.

Bathroom Safety Checklist
⬦ Cover all electrical outlets with child-safe covers. Install cord protectors.

⬦ Lower water temperature to a maximum of 120°F (48.89°C). Teach your child which knob is for cold water and which is for hot and how to adjust the water temperature before wetting her hands.

⬦ Shop electrical appliances, such as hair dryers, curling irons and shavers, unplugged and out of reach. Keep electric toothbrush chargers out of reach.

⬦ Install childproof latches or locks on drawers that contain toiletries, solutions, medications, vitamins, razors, scissors and other hazards, or keep them in another room.

⬦ Put nonskid mats in baths and showers. Cover bath taps with soft protectors.

⬦ Put nonskid mats under rugs.

⬦ Purchase all medications and health products (such as mouthwash and cold medicine) in childproof containers, and keep them locked up or out of reach. Keep in mind that surprisingly young children can often figure out how to open childproof containers, so keeping them up or locked is important.

⬦ Use plastic or paper cups and soap holders, not glass.

⬦ Pay attention to what is put in the bathroom bin, as curious children are known to explore this container. Razor blades, medications, cleaning supplies, hair colour products and other dangerous items should not be thrown away in the bathroom.

◇ Remove the plastic or rubber end caps on doorstops or replace them with safer one-piece designs to avoid a choking hazard.

◇ Remove any decorative items that could be potential choking hazards.

◇ Secure any cabinets, dressers or other freestanding furniture, as they pose a climbing or tipping danger.

◇ Install ground-fault circuit interrupters (GFCI or GFI) on outlets. These safety devices are designed to protect from electrical shock. They turn off the current flowing to the plug if there is an electrical problem, such as a wet cord plugged into it. Test your GFIs as often as recommended by the manufacturer (typically monthly) by pressing a test or reset button.

◇ Keep cigarettes, matches, lighters and ashtrays out of children's reach.

◇ Make sure your child's potty, seat insert and footstool are securely in place. Keep in mind that these can be used as a climbing device to get your child up to explore higher places.

◇ Install metal window safety guards on all upper-floor windows. (Screens do not prevent falling accidents.)

◇ Shorten curtain or blind cords so they are out of reach.

◇ Keep a backup key handy in case your child locks herself in the bathroom.

Mother-Speak

"We were visiting my mother-in-law and Jessie went off to the bathroom. I was busy helping to prepare dinner but suddenly realized that he'd been gone quite a long time. I found him in the bathroom, happily sorting all of Grandma's pills in colourful little piles. We had no idea if he'd put any of them into his mouth, so we had to spend a tense and frightening night at the hospital while his vital signs were monitored. It turns out that he didn't take any of the pills, but it was still one of the scariest days of my life."

—Karen, mother of three-year-old Jessie

⟡ The toilet bowl is like an open bucket of water—it is a drowning hazard. If you have younger children in the house, or young children who visit, keep the bathroom door closed with a childproof knob, or install a toilet seat latch. (These can be opened by an older child or an adult but not a toddler or a baby.)

⟡ Accompany your child whenever he uses bathrooms away from home, including in public toilets and family homes—counting grandparents' homes, too. Many people have poisonous products, medications without childproof caps, electrical hazards, and any number of other safety hazards you may be unaware of.

⟡ Pay attention to any hazards brought into your home by guests, who may put medications or other dangerous items on the counters or in the waste-basket.

◇ Install smoke detectors and change batteries regularly.

◇ Install a childproof night-light that is cool to the touch.

◇ Vacuum or sweep the bathroom floor frequently.

◇ Learn first aid and CPR. Classes are available through agencies such as the Red Cross and St John Ambulance. Keep emergency phone numbers written down on or near your telephones.

◇ If your child spends time at nursery or with a child-minder, a babysitter, a grandparent or anyone else, insist that safety guidelines are followed in that environment also.

◇ Your entire home—not just your bathroom—should be safe for your child. Consider hiring a specialized company to help you childproof your home.

Index

About the Author

Parenting educator Elizabeth Pantley is president of Better Beginnings, Inc., a family resource and education company. Elizabeth frequently speaks to parents at schools, hospitals and parent groups around the world. Her presentations are received with enthusiasm and are praised as realistic, warm and helpful.

She is a regular radio show guest and is frequently quoted as a parenting expert in newspapers and magazines such as *Parents, Parenting, Woman's Day, Good Housekeeping* and *Redbook* and on hundreds of parent-directed websites. She publishes a newsletter, *Parent Tips*, that is distributed in schools. She is the author of these parenting books, available in eighteen languages:

- *The No-Cry Sleep Solution: Gentle Ways to Help Your Baby Sleep Through the Night*
- *The No-Cry Sleep Solution for Toddlers and Preschoolers: Gentle Ways to Stop Bedtime Battles and Improve Your Child's Sleep*
- *Gentle Baby Care: No-Cry, No-Fuss, No-Worry— Essential Tips for Raising Your Baby*
- *Hidden Messages: What Our Words and Actions Are Really Telling Our Children*
- *Perfect Parenting: The Dictionary of 1,000 Parenting Tips*
- *Kid Cooperation: How to Stop Yelling, Nagging and Pleading & Get Kids to Cooperate*

- *The No-Cry Discipline Solution: Gentle Ways to Promote Good Behavior and Stop the Whining, Tantrums, and Tears* (coming in 2007)

Elizabeth was a contributing author to *The Successful Child* by Dr. William and Martha Sears.

Elizabeth and her husband, Robert, live in the state of Washington, along with their four children (Angela, Vanessa, David and Coleton), Grama (Elizabeth's mother), and assorted family pets. Elizabeth is an involved participant in her children's school and sports activities and has served in positions as varied as softball coach and school PTA president.

www.pantley.com